PRODUCT OF ITALY, MADE IN CANADA

An Immigrant's Love Letter to Food, Family, and Resilience

ALSO BY ROSANNA MICELOTTA BATTIGELLI

Historical Fiction

La Brigantessa

Short Fiction

Pigeon Soup & Other Stories

Children's Books

Pumpkin Orange, Pumpkin Round

Easter Morning, Easter Sun

Harlequin Romances

Swept Away by the Enigmatic Tycoon

Captivated by Her Italian Boss

Caribbean Escape with the Tycoon

Falling for the Sardinian Baron

Rescued by the Guarded Tycoon

Reunited with the Tycoon Next Door

PRODUCT OF ITALY, MADE IN CANADA

An Immigrant's Love Letter to Food, Family, and Resilience

Rosanna Micelotta Battigelli

Library and Archives Canada Cataloguing in Publication

Title: Product of Italy, made in Canada : an immigrant's love letter to food, family, and resilience / by Rosanna Micelotta Battigelli.
Names: Battigelli, Rosanna, author
Identifiers: Canadiana (print) 20250196565 | Canadiana (ebook) 20250196573 | ISBN 9781988989983 (softcover) | ISBN 9781988989990 (EPUB)
Subjects: LCSH: Battigelli, Rosanna. | LCGFT: Creative nonfiction. | LCGFT: Essays.
Classification: LCC PS8553.A8334 P76 2025 | DDC C814/.6—dc23

Printed and bound in Canada on 100% recycled paper.
Editor: Randall Perry
Cover Design: Sabrina Futia
Author photo: Westmount Photography

Published by:
Latitude 46 Publishing
info@latitude46publishing.com
Latitude46publishing.com

We acknowledge the support of the Ontario Arts Council and the Canada Book Fund for their generous financial support.

To my family, immediate and extended,
for your love and support.

To my dear students, with whom I have
shared my love of learning and creativity.

“There is a thin line that separates laughter and pain, comedy and tragedy, humor and hurt.”
—Erma Bombeck

“You never know how strong you are, until being strong is your only choice.”
—Bob Marley

The Immigrants, 1963

Assunta's eyes fluttered open at the first sound. She turned her head to look at the two-month-old baby lying next to her on the bed, eyes still closed and tiny mouth contorting in preparation for his second, much louder cry for attention.

Was it feeding time already? Assunta felt around for the clock on the night table and squinted at it in the darkened room. Almost midnight. Just the beginning. This baby was not like the others, allowing her the luxury of five to six hours between feedings. No, Cosimo was a demanding infant, insatiable it seemed, with a three-to-four-hour limit between each feeding. Around the clock. Positioning Cosimo in the crook of her arm while still lying on the bed, she whispered, "Shhh," and began to nurse him.

Cosimo. He had started life in a new land—America—a land that would be his from the beginning. And maybe to the finish. Assunta felt a familiar prickle under her eyelids, and a wave of emotion that seemed to settle in her chest like a wooden barrel, crushing her heart and spirit.

What spirit? a voice inside her demanded. As the tears began to squeeze out from Assunta's closed lids, trickling in warm streaks down her cheeks, she tried to pinpoint when she had lost her spirit.

Was it when she and Nicola realized there was no future for them working the land in southern Italy? When she'd said her last goodbye to her parents, relatives, and friends? When Nicola had shown her the cramped three-room apartment in Gatchell, where they would live while he tried to find work in Sudbury?

Assunta squeezed her eyes tightly to stem the flow of tears, and then gently adjusted the position of the baby. She had to be strong. For all of them.

Her eyes shifted to the two cots across the room. Under one blanket, two mounds slept soundly. Her girls, Giuseppina and Rosanna. Two-year-old Pasquale was sleeping in the corner cot.

Nicola should be back soon. He had been asked to do a two-day janitorial stint to cover for his friend Stefano, who was ill. Today was his last day and Nicola was doing a double shift. Assunta felt a familiar knot of anxiety in her chest. Since their arrival in Canada three months ago, her anxiety had escalated daily with Nicola's every unsuccessful attempt at finding work. He never had to say anything—the news was stamped on his face every evening when he walked through the door: mouth pursed in a thin line; eyebrows furrowed under clouded, disillusioned eyes; shoulders sagging. Assunta would look up expectantly when she heard the door handle turning, and seconds later, the hope in her heart would dissipate instantly as her eyes met his. Embracing him, she would hide her disappointment, for allowing him to see her growing despair would only be an extra weight to the burden he already shouldered.

She was always thankful for the distraction the children provided. At the sound of their precious papa's entry, they would rush to greet him, inundating him with hugs and kisses that made him smile and appeared to resuscitate his wounded spirit. Nicola would play with them in the living room while Assunta prepared supper—usually a simple meal of pasta and beans, or broth with bread she would bake when Cosimo was sleeping.

God help us, she would pray silently as she cooked. *Thank you for the abundance of another meal, another day of grace. And healthy children.*

❧

Last night, Nicola broke the news to Assunta when the children were asleep. Nicola sat on the side of the bed with Assunta. Taking her hand, he stroked it pensively before saying quietly, "We have to move, Assunta."

Assunta's eyes widened at the implication of his words. The fact that he had uttered them so softly emphasized their gravity. She bit her lip, feeling numb, and gazed past Nicola's head to the window. Slowly she rose and walked toward it, cringing at the sound of the wooden floorboards beneath her feet. Old Mr.

Renzetti down below was probably complaining to his wife this very minute, she thought, about the "upstairs noise."

She had spotted him from this window once, out in the front yard with his wife, raking up mounds of faded oak leaves on the lawn. Through the window's three air holes, Assunta had heard him saying, quite distinctly, that they were a nice family, but that the children made too much noise with their jumping and running around.

Assunta hated being in an upstairs apartment with four children. The effort of trying to keep them quiet all the time, so as not to disturb the landlord and his wife, was getting to her.

Oh, she was grateful to Mr. and Mrs. Renzetti for renting them the apartment. However, Assunta found herself often daydreaming about the house she had left behind in the old country. A simple stone dwelling that had been her grandmother's, with russet roof tiles and a terrace that looked over the distant hills and valleys to the strip of darker blue that marked the infinite stretch of the Ionian Sea. It could make you feel like you were on top of the world.

Assunta gazed at the snowflakes spiraling downward like feathers onto the sea of white already covering the ground. It was strange to see the land buried in this way. She wondered if she would ever get used to it. And the cold.

Shivering, she riveted her gaze back to Nicola. "Why?"

"The old man can't take the noise."

"*O Dio,* they're just being children."

"I know. But it's harder for older people. I don't like it, but I understand it."

Nicola joined Assunta at the window. "Look, they're not turning us out overnight. We have a few weeks..."

ꝺ

Assunta reached for a handkerchief to stem a fresh flow of tears as she recalled Nicola's words from the night before. Her blurred gaze fell on the note that Nicola had left on his pillow:

> *I didn't want to wake you, amore. Please don't worry. Today is a new day. I didn't bring you and the children to a new country to be hungry and homeless. Have faith. I'll be home around midnight. Give our beautiful bambini lots of kisses for me. Nicola.*

Assunta had made it through the day, reading Nicola's note every time a doubt or fear attempted to take root in her mind. And after Giuseppina, Rosanna, and Pasquale went to bed, she lay next to Cosimo and closed her eyes with the intent of resting a few minutes before clearing off the table and doing the dishes. But the few minutes had stretched into almost four hours. It was past midnight now.

At the sound of footsteps, Assunta rose from the bed, draped a sweater over her nightgown, and tiptoed into the kitchen to turn on the light for Nicola.

A moment later, he was inside, his hat and coat heavily dusted with snow. Assunta walked toward him slowly, her eyes swollen. Her dark brown hair was tousled, tumbling over her shoulders. He gazed at her for a few seconds, the snow on his hat and coat melting along with his heart.

She stopped a foot away from him, about to give him the usual embrace, and then she froze. Nicola's mouth wasn't pursed. His eyebrows weren't drawn together. His shoulders weren't sagging. And his eyes were bright, not at all discouraged.

"I found us a place," he whispered, smiling. "It's four blocks away from here, on Walter Street, and it's not an upstairs apartment." He watched the play of emotions on Assunta's face at his words, and then added, "My friend Stefano gave my name to his foreman at the smelter in Copper Cliff. They're looking to hire. I have a meeting with him tomorrow. And tomorrow night we're going to celebrate. Let's forget about beans and order a porchetta from Gatchell Meat Market. And the day after tomorrow there's going to be a spaghetti supper in St. Anthony's Church basement.

"It's time we met some of our neighbours around here and made some friends, don't you think?"

Assunta was silent for a moment, and then gave a shout of elation, not caring if all the children woke up, or even if Mr. Renzetti woke up and banged his cane on the ceiling. She flung her sweater in the air, and Nicola, laughing, swung her around.

Assunta caught a glimpse of the snow swirling outside the window. And beyond the rooftops, the Inco stack, a beacon of hope for Nicola and for all of them. Maybe she could get used to snow, she thought, smiling.

Christmas 1963 was going to be the start of a new life in Sudbury. Thanks to God... and *Cristoforo Colombo.*

Product Of Italy, Made In Canada

In April 1963, Canada was not our *Canada. Canada was a place where our ship landed, unloaded the lot of us out at Pier 21, and rested its ample body on the cool blue sheets of the Atlantic before puffing its way back to Italy. The mighty* Saturnia*—how many immigrants traveled nestled within its ribcage during its lifetime? Felt its heart beating along with theirs, felt it heaving with every breath of the capricious wind.*

She wishes she could recall the trip itself—her one and only transatlantic journey. But she was only three. Over the years, she has strained to remember something, anything. She wonders, why is memory so important as one gets older? Why is there such a desire to retrieve memories of the past, of the minute details of life, of the evidence of one's existence on this planet? The only memory she can recall of that time, and it is fleeting, is of being in a very large space with a man—her father—and waiting. Waiting to see a movie on the ship? Waiting to enter the dining room? She'll never know for sure.

We took the train from Halifax to Montreal, where we visited some of my mother's cousins, who graciously put us up for two nights. We were five: my mother, my father, older sister, younger brother, me. Then the journey west to Ontario, then to the northern mining town of Sudbury, our final stop, where my mother's brother had already settled and was working at the International Nickel Company—Inco—where my father would eventually find work, too.

The Canadian landscape in May did not please her mother, whose heartstrings were still attached to Italy. They trailed her everywhere like a lost puppy, tangling her emotions like a fallen ball of yarn. It took her a long time to get used to Canada, to northern Ontario, with its short growing season and its seemingly endless winters of swirling blizzards, waist-high snowdrifts, and freezing rain.

Her parents had risked everything and left their homeland to find work in the land of opportunity. The land that had attracted them, and thousands of others, to the possibility of a better life. A land with different languages, different customs, different dreams. Dreams for their children to have more than they did.

My life as a Canadian didn't officially begin until I received my Canadian citizenship at the age of nine. My first memory of life in Canada is of being in a kindergarten classroom. I remember feeling completely alone and different. I was unable to understand my teacher. She didn't speak my language and couldn't understand me. It was a rude awakening. I was in Canada, but Canada wasn't mine.

Of course, she eventually learned to speak English. She gobbled up the words she was taught, instinctively knowing, perhaps, that words were the key to fitting in. Belonging. Being like the others. But fitting in wasn't easy. At home, her parents spoke to her in their Calabrese dialect, cooked the way they always did, raised her and her sister and brothers the way they would have in the old country. They made friends with the other Italian immigrants on their street and in their neighbourhood. When their parents could afford to buy a modest house, they continued their tradition of gardening.

Our Canada was "Little Italy." Our Canadian garden had tomatoes, zucchini, eggplants, peas, beans, broccoli, and dandelions. Pomodori, zucchini, melanzane, piselli, fagioli, rapini, e cicoria... everything we could imagine from the Italy of old. Our parents continued to cling to their other traditions: making tomato preserves and wine in the fall, "chinuli" pastries at Christmas, pork sausages in January, sweet "cuzzupi" pastries at Easter. Oh, the sights and the smells! All those bushels of shiny tomatoes, their skins glistening; the sweet aroma of fresh tomato sauce, bubbling away with fresh, green sprigs of basilico; the musky fermenting smell of the zinfandel, muscat, and alicante grapes; the first taste of the pan-fried pork sausages sprinkled with pepper and fennel seed. Our Canada was spaghetti and polpette (meatballs), riso e patate, brodo (chicken soup), melanzane ripiene (stuffed eggplant).

Unlike their parents, who favoured the foods they had always known, she and her siblings embraced the strangeness of Canadian food. They desperately wanted to try peanut butter and jam sandwiches instead of panini with mortadella and provolone cheese. They wanted to live more like *Canadians*. They were happy to go skating at the neighbourhood rink and to eat French fries and hot dogs at Bell Park by Ramsey Lake in the summer.

But, of course, we come full circle. We return to the traditions we were taught. Now, as adults, we buy mortadella and panini for our children. We try out our mother's old recipes, the ones we had to write down, while she spent her lifetime cooking with a pinch of this or a handful of that. Farina quanto basta. Zucchero quanto basta. We enroll our children in Italian lessons. We want our Canadian children to appreciate our heritage, their heritage.

She knows her children love Canada. It is *their* land. It was always their land, right from the start. She has come to love Canada also. But she will never forget *l'Italia bella.* Like many immigrants, she will always remember her homeland with nostalgia, and she will return to her welcoming arms as often as she can, bringing back pictures of her golden beaches, turquoise seas, silver-green olive groves, magnificent cathedrals, picturesque piazzas. Pictures to keep her memories alive. Pictures she didn't have when she first came to Canada.

And when we're sitting with our caffè latte, recalling our recent visit to the old country, we realize just how Canadian we are, proud and tall like the Rockies, flexible like Prairie wheat, solid like the Canadian Shield. We are *Canada.*

Product of Italy. Made in Canada!

Canada is ours. Like the words of the song we heard in school years ago, before some of us could even understand the words, "This land was made for you and me."

You Are What You… Wear

I am three years old and frowning as I sit for the official passport picture prior to our immigration to Canada in the spring of 1963. In the framed picture sitting atop the antique sewing machine my mother gave me years ago, I observe my mother's flawless complexion and serene gaze. I wonder about the emotions that must have been churning just below the surface at the decision to leave her homeland with her husband and three children (and another on the way) and embark upon a nine-day ocean journey to America. She must have wondered how long it would be before she'd see her family or homeland again.

I am flanked by my siblings: my older sister Giuseppina (Pina for short) and my younger brother Pasquale. I am the quintessential "middle child," although I won't hold this position for very long, with my mother at the end of her second trimester. Her fourth child will be born in Canada.

My sister's five-year-old expression mirrors our mother's calm demeanour. Pina is slender, almost skinny, and darker-skinned than me. I have inherited my mother's fair skin. I'm not fat, but my bones are amply padded. My face is round, with cheeks that I'm sure delighted relatives and friends in Italy, with their rotund pinchability. My one-year-old brother, Pasquale, seems reasonably content in the photo, biting into a chocolate bar.

Am I scowling because *he* got one and I didn't? Or did I finish mine already, and want the remainder of his?

My appetite was never an issue when I was a child, my mother often told me. Unlike my willowy sister, I ate heartily when Ma encouraged us: "*Mangia! Mangia!*" From the start, I made my mother very happy with my ready acceptance of her offerings, such as her oversized biscotti and meatballs. Everything seemed to swell during the cooking process, and I inevitably swelled afterwards.

Given my lifelong love of good food, it is reasonable to assume that my infantile pouting in the photo is directly connected to issues around the chocolate bar. However, I can't discount a second theory, that clothes had something to do with it.

My outfit in the photo is only partially visible: a light knit sweater with a rounded collar, edged with a dark border. It looks nice enough. But there *is* one item that I am wearing that may have been the cause of my trauma.

The bow.

It is resting in my hair, pristine white against my shiny dark locks.

I didn't like bows. In fact, I *detested* them. As captured by childhood photos and my memories, my mother insisted on tying them in my hair from the time that I had enough hair to hold them in place. Perhaps they tugged on my sensitive scalp. To this day I cannot explain the reason for my aversion to them.

My earliest childhood memories revolve around "things" my mother made me wear on my head or elsewhere on my body. My mother was an accomplished seamstress, having learned the art from her mother. Sewing, knitting, embroidery, crocheting—she acquired these skills as a *signorina*, preparing her for her eventual role as a wife and mother. Ma put her talents to good use to protect her family from the harsh Canadian winters. She wasted no time knitting up a storm. She bedecked us all with wool hats, mittens, sweaters, and socks. Instead of being grateful, I threw a tantrum over the wool hat she insisted I wear. I felt I looked ridiculous in it, and I was only six.

My mother would pull the hat snugly over my forehead and then tie it securely under my chin. Not only did the hat outline the perfect roundness of my head, concealing my short hair and emphasizing the equal roundness of my face, it was topped by an oversized pompom. (My mother's meatballs weren't the only things oversized!)

The bottom line is that I felt self-conscious at the age of six. Imagine! Incidentally, my brother is wearing a wool hat in the passport picture; however, it lacks a pompom. How did *he* get to be so lucky?

"What a brat!" you may be thinking... such a fuss over a simple wool hat, pompom or not. And to cause untold grief to a mother who had probably stayed up for hours, knitting and sewing for her kids as they were all nestled snug in their beds, while visions of spumoni danced in their heads.

Brat indeed. But perhaps it was a middle-child thing. A subconscious desire to become the centre of attention...

I had been the middle child until my brother Cosimo was born but losing that status must have had additional implications. Obviously, then, I needed even *more* attention. This all makes perfect sense to me now: I protested all outward things like pompoms, hair bows, and clothes, when it was really all about my inner state. (Perhaps I should have pursued studies in psychology.)

My tantrum even resulted in a bleeding nose on one occasion. I had obviously burst a gasket. My mother proceeded to use an old-country technique to stop the flow. She had me tilt my head forward into the bathroom sink so she could pour cold water over my neck. I never verified the effectiveness of this procedure with a doctor in my adult years, but it worked on me at the time. Maybe it was the shock of the icy water touching my heated skin that stopped the blood in its tracks.

Ma calmly washed my face, dried my neck, bundled me up in my coat, placed the offensive wool hat unceremoniously back on my head, tied it firmly under my quivering chin, and sent me off to school a mere two streets away. As I plodded down the street, the pompom poised on my head like a triumphant beacon, I waited until the "Ice Queen" was out of view, then I untied the hat, whisked it off my head, and stuck it in my school bag.

You can imagine the complexities within the invisible triangle that included my mother, my clothes, and me. One day in Grade 7, I wore a new pair of pants that my mother had made me. They were light brown with intersecting lines of green and red throughout. They *looked* nice. I didn't realize until I was well on my way to school that I was wearing 100 per cent pure wool: the fabric from hell. Perhaps it was the friction of the wool rubbing against my thighs that drove me to near insanity. I'm not sure—the laws of physics and thermodynamics have always escaped me—but I do know that I could not concentrate on anything else that day at school.

Have you ever had an itch and couldn't scratch? Pure torture. My legs itched all day. I squirmed frequently. I recall asking the teacher for permission to go to the washroom several times. I had no real relief, however, until I ran home after school and tore the pants off. My legs were covered in a pink rash.

I swore I'd never wear the pants again, and I tried to convince my mother that the pants were killing me, that they ranked up there with some of the most horrific medieval torture devices in history. "*Come sei esagerata!*" she said in our Calabrese dialect. "Stop being such a drama queen!" She suggested that I wear panty hose under the pants, since they had no liner. I reluctantly consented, hoping she was right. What I discovered the next time I wore them was that panty hose under pure wool did not eliminate the itching but increased it.

I thought I was going to die! I envisioned the headline: TEENAGER DIES FROM TOXIC MIX OF HOSE AND WOOL—MOTHER DEVASTATED. I swore that never again would I wear wool pants and panty hose together.

If I didn't throw a tantrum over some item of clothing when I was young, then I fainted. Well, maybe I'm exaggerating somewhat. I only resorted to a tantrum when I felt something was causing me extreme physical oppression or discomfort, such as the abominable pompom crushing my soft head. And there were only two incidents of fainting, both of which were genuine. I was not a proficient actor.

The first episode occurred during my First Communion, the holiest of occasions. I was seven, and by this tender age I had settled into a daily cycle of culinary contentedness, anticipating the southern Italian dishes that my mother might prepare: *pasta al forno*, stuffed eggplant, breaded veal cutlets, and such.

I wasn't fat, but *bella robusta,* as more than one well-meaning relative put it. Perhaps I also helped myself to whatever my sister left on her plate at mealtimes. At the end of the day, her cheekbones were clearly delineated, while mine were snug under the quilts of my cheeks.

And what a sight when you add a generous sprinkling of freckles and a puffy mound of ringlets. Ma had insisted I wear Italian curlers to bed the night before this sacred event so my hair would be perfect for the photo session, and she even had me wear them in school the next day. I was sent off with narrow pink curlers studding my head, along with several other girls, all of us daughters of Italian immigrants. I tried to ignore the pointing and chuckles of some of the boys and older students in the schoolyard and couldn't wait for the bell to ring so I could at least be in my own classroom.

At home after school, my mother helped me into the voluminous Communion dress she had made me. It resembled more a miniature wedding gown than something to wear for Communion, replete with yards of intricate lace around the neck, wrists, and skirt, and a crinoline underskirt that made the dress puff out—like I needed additional puffing! Since our family didn't own a car, my uncle Peter drove us to the photographer's studio. Looking at the photos years later, I couldn't help thinking that I resembled a real "Southern belle" as I stood beaming.

But I wasn't beaming with pleasure, as you can imagine. My face was beaded with sweat from the glare of the photographer's lamp, under which I feared I would soon melt, or vanish, like something out of *Lost in Space,* my favourite television show.

My head had not escaped adornment, either. I wore a crown of thorns around which hung a scratchy, shroud-like veil. It certainly felt like thorns; perhaps it was meant to have that effect, seeing as how I was becoming the metaphorical bride of Christ. And Christ, did I suffer! The crown sticking into my head, the lace picking at and lacerating my delicate skin, the snug bodice constraining my heaving chest, the clinging white leotards, the pinching new white shoes, the weight of layer after layer of billowing skirt, not to mention layer after layer of snake-like ringlets. All this suffering invoked thoughts of that dreaded state we were taught to fear at school: hell and all its accompanying tortures!

My mother seemed quite happy with the creation that had taken her countless hours, days, and weeks to complete. She was smiling at me, encouraging me to smile for the photographer, but I found it hard to comply, especially after catching sight of myself in a full-length mirror. I looked like a round, rosy-cheeked, multi-layered, three-foot-tall cake-top decoration.

I felt hot and weak. I had no energy to throw a tantrum; something I'd never dare in public. Instead, I heaved a big sigh—like Christ, I imagine, giving up the ghost—and promptly fainted.

In retrospect, my Communion dress was a work of art, my mother's *pièce de résistance.* I only wish she hadn't sent it off years later to a niece in Italy. I look at my Communion photo every so often and never fail to marvel at my mother's remarkable sewing talents. I didn't appreciate these talents when I was seven, sweltering in the photo studio, but I certainly can now.

My second fainting spell occurred in the summer after I completed Grade 8. My mother wanted me to try on the uniform she was making me for my entry into an all-girl Catholic high school. It was identical to what would have come from the store, but my mother had saved a bundle sewing it herself.

She pinned the hem while I tried to stand motionless. The fact that we were in the middle of a heatwave and I found it hard to breathe may have been a factor in my resulting loss of consciousness. Maybe it was the subconscious fear that she would insist I wear a bow in my hair on the first day of school—a bow that she would make with some of the leftover material. Or maybe make me sleep done up with the tight Italian curlers of my childhood.

I never fainted again, but toward the end of my last year in high school, there was another clothing incident.

"Ma, you don't have to make me a dress for the semi-formal," I told her tentatively one Friday night. I had grown up with clothes she had made me. I wanted to splurge and treat myself to a store-bought dress this time. "I've saved some money," I added, anxious to reassure her that she wouldn't have to pay for it.

My mother's brows furrowed, and I waited anxiously. Would she insist? She could be decisive and quick. If she agreed, it would be going against her natural inclination.

"Go 'head," she said in her broken English. *Go ahead.* Her features relaxed and so did I. Who'd have thought that she would agree instantly? I could only assume that she welcomed the break.

I took the bus downtown the next day. With a sense of freedom and anticipation, I glided from one rack to another in a popular boutique, choosing a few gowns to try on. I finally decided on a floor-length black number with a diaphanous bolero-type jacket over a sleek bodice and flowing skirt. It made me feel sensuous, like the innocent yet sultry Harlequin romance heroines I loved to read about. And I got it on sale! I brought it home, expecting approval from my mother; after all, it wasn't low-cut or anything. I pulled it out of the bag, smiling.

"*Ritornala domani,*" she ordered, her face and voice grim.

My cheeks started to burn. "Why should I return it? What's the matter with it? I like it."

"You only wear black when someone dies." She pursed her lips. "You're bringing this back to the store tomorrow. Get yourself another dress. This one will bring bad luck."

I was speechless. Ma was superstitious, as were most people I knew from the old country, but this was going too far. We were in Canada, not the mountainside village of Camini in Calabria. I wasn't about to adhere to this ancient belief. I insisted that I was going to keep the dress.

My mother burst into tears. This was the second time I had ever seen her cry, and it shook me. After assuring her that I would return the dress, I retreated to my room, upset and confused. Although I had tried to assert myself initially, my sensitive nature did not permit me to cause my mother any more grief.

Reluctant though I was to part with the dusky black dress, I eventually found another one that I liked just as much. It was red and black and had a Flamenco-like style to it. My mother nodded when I held it up for her approval. Black was acceptable if combined with another colour, and this dress had wide alternating red and black diagonal bands with a bottom ruffle. I had to grudgingly admit to myself that the first dress was a bit too, well, mature for me.

My mother continued to sew outfits for me, and I still have many of them hanging in one of my closets. They are a testimonial to her prowess and patience as a seamstress. I've donated lots of clothes to charities, but I can't bear to part with my mother's creations.

There's the flaming red, spaghetti-strap satin dress she made me when I was engaged. It was hot! And there is the burgundy wool (yes, wool!) two-piece suit she made for me when I started teaching in the early 80s—lined, of course. Then there's the delicate, blue-flowered summer dress with ivory satin waistband and trimming that made me feel like Princess Diana.

Each dress holds a story within its seams. A story of immigrant dreams and challenges in a new country. A story about adjustment to a new language and culture while clinging to the comforting traditions of the old country. A story of countless spools of multi-coloured thread serged and stitched with love through layers of lace, wool, and a myriad of other fabrics that make up the tapestry of my life, and my relationship with my mother.

I never learned to sew like her. Other than sewing a basic hem and re-attaching buttons, I remain sewing-challenged. My mother attempted to teach me years ago, but the knots on my threads always tended to be clumsy and oversized. I was relieved when she gave up on me, and she probably felt just as relieved.

Ma, in her own way, allowed me to grow, not with a needle in my hand but with a pen and pencil, so I could eventually stitch words and sentences together, hemming in thoughts and memories to create a multi-layered story with pompoms, wool, and all the trimmings.

I finish dusting the passport picture in its gilded frame and set it back on my mother's "New Stanley Mills" sewing machine that helped create clothes for my siblings and me.

My mother is gone now, but I'm sure she's looking down from her sewing room in heaven, having finished a couple of angel dresses, and is just about ready to start making spaghetti and meatballs for some of our family up there.

And some extra-large ones for the Big Guy.

Angel Of God

Death visited our family and enveloped us in a tight embrace of its dark cloak on a dismal April day in 1975. I was fifteen years old. I arrived home from high school as usual, wondering why there were so many parked cars near our house. I went around to the back entrance and was surprised to see my home full of people. They were all friends I recognized, *paesani*, who lived in the same, predominantly Italian, neighbourhood. Only this time they were not smiling.

Grim faces turned to look at me. I scanned the kitchen, and then further into the living room, looking for my mother or father. I suddenly realized that someone was crying, sobbing... deep, tortured gasps that I had never heard before. My eyes focused on the shaking figure hunched over in the living room chair—my mother. At that moment, she lifted her hands away from her face and reached for me.

"*A figghia mia; sinda jìu a nostra Pina,*" she sobbed. "Our Giuseppina has gone away!"

I was stunned for a moment; I didn't know what she meant. Why was my mother in such a state? Where had my older sister, Pina, gone? Wasn't she still in the hospital?

Days earlier, my worried parents had brought Pina to see the doctor. Stomach flu was the diagnosis, so they brought her back home, expecting the symptoms to eventually pass. When Pina developed severe cramps, they immediately rushed her to the hospital emergency department. Her appendix had ruptured, they were told, and she needed immediate surgery. I accompanied my parents to the hospital, where Pina was recovering, the next day.

That was just yesterday, I thought, confused. Then my mother repeated her words, and the stark truth hit me. Pina was dead. That was the reason all these people were here. I held my mother's hand, helpless, as she told me that the poison had gotten into Pina's blood. Peritonitis consumed her delicate body at seventeen years of age, all within a span of one week.

My father, always a strong, hard-working figure, seemed a broken man standing nearby, his body sagging with silent grief, his face etched with tears of helplessness. The stark scene that remains in my mind is that of the total despair and pain of my mother as she wept: "*Pina mia, o Pina mia. Ti pighiaru pur 'a tia. Che dolore, che dolore.*" My mother's older sister Anna Rosa had died when she was eighteen. "They took you, too," she wailed. "Oh, the pain. The pain!"

I remember someone trying to give my mother some food that evening, telling her she had to eat to be strong, but she refused. From the disjointed cries around me, I understood that a friend called Teresa, who had acted as Pina's sponsor at Confirmation, was going to be responsible for getting a burial dress.

"What a tragedy!" I heard someone whisper.

"It was God's will," a close elderly friend of the family murmured repeatedly to try to console my mother, who, hours later, was still in the same chair, her eyes red and swollen, her pain no less numbed.

I remember the rest of the evening as a blur, except for the absence of my younger brothers, who were picked up directly after school and stayed with my aunt and uncle and cousins that night. I was asked if I wanted to join them.

"Ti spagni u stai sula?"

It was the room I had always shared with Pina... I didn't understand why I should feel afraid. I stayed there that night and for the nights to come, although sometimes I slept in my mother's bed when my father was working night shifts at the smelter. On those nights, my mother couldn't sleep alone.

The small neighbourhood where we lived was shocked by the news, as was the Catholic high school in which Pina had been in Grade 11 and I in Grade 10. At the funeral home, hordes of people came to express their condolences to my family. The two adjoining rooms streamed with people, young and old. My parents wept inconsolably as they sat by Pina's coffin. She looked like a life-sized porcelain doll.

"*Un angelo di Dio,*" someone murmured nearby. I remember laying a rose next to her pale, lifeless hands, into which a rosary had been placed. An angel of God.

The day of the funeral was dark and bleak and rainy.

"I hope this is not one of those typical Italian funerals, with all that wailing and crying," commented a girl in Pina's class. Her home room class, along with several teachers, had come to the funeral Mass.

What cold, insensitive words, I thought as I followed my grieving parents up the aisle. Surely crying was not an act exclusive to Italians. Fortunately, there were kind, supportive friends to ease the slap of those words, although for some time I could not look at the girl at school without feeling a knot of bitterness.

The day after Pina's funeral, my mother's cousin came over and filled the kitchen sink with deep black dye. The mixture swallowed up my mother's light-coloured clothes and the heavy night rain pelted the window above the sink, mirroring the black undulations of the dye working through the fabric. As each article of clothing underwent its funereal metamorphosis and was subsequently wrung out and hung to dry on a clothesline in the basement, I wondered if Canadian families went through this ritual, or if they just went out and bought black clothing for the mourning period. I expected it would be the latter, if they did indeed have such a custom. I instinctively understood that my mother, who was most adept in using her refined sewing skills in clothing herself and her family, wasn't about to start spending money on new clothes for herself. From the time the dyed clothes were ready, my mother wore black to mark her grief, as was the custom she grew up with.

The one-year period of *lutto*—mourning—in our household was a long one. At least I thought it felt unbearably so at the time, given the limited understanding of adolescence. Only much later, when blessed with children of my own, could I fathom the meaning of such a loss. I could understand how devastated my parents must have felt, how painful it must have been to carry on the responsibility of raising their three remaining children.

I no longer had a sister. The pink room we had shared was now mine. I remember quiet moments, strange moments, like helping to pack away her belongings and her clothes. I recall finding a letter that filled me with anguish; it was a letter to Pina from a boy admirer that I had hidden from her in adolescent insensitivity. How I wished I could have taken that moment back, had shown more kindness.

The television set remained off for an entire year. There would be no singing or laughing in our home, my mother told us sorrowfully. The radio was eventually turned on, but only for the news or the weather report. At times I thought life was overly harsh, although I didn't have any previous experience with which to compare it. Canadian mourning customs were foreign to me; up until that time I had never attended a funeral or even visited a funeral home.

I felt lonely. I didn't have many friends over during the grieving period. I don't remember sharing my feelings about my home life with anyone. Perhaps I felt different, vulnerable to what people who didn't share my culture would say or think. I was sad that I couldn't attend school dances or other social activities. Meals were solemn, with little talk. I longed for the time when things could be normal, and I could laugh at home again without feeling guilty.

My parents turned to devout prayer and the solace they found in the Church to help them cope with the tragedy. Eventually they began to smile and then laugh once again. I recall cheering inwardly when I heard that first laugh, a sign that my parents could allow themselves to be happy. My brothers Pasquale and Cosimo, who were thirteen and eleven, respectively, sat in front of the television for hours after its one-year moratorium was lifted. I joined them with a sense of relief that life would continue normally once again.

As the years passed, I realized that Pina's death had made my mother even more protective of me. I did not participate in many social activities. I had friends in the neighbourhood, but I didn't venture far from home. I didn't want to add to my mother's worries after all she had been through, losing a daughter. Occasionally, I resented the restrictions; I saw myself as being different from other Canadians. As an immigrant, I was sometimes embarrassed that my parents weren't more like Canadian parents, who seemed more permissive and less protective of their daughters. Again, looking back, I can appreciate their fears, their concerns, and their expectations.

I have come to realize that everyone mourns in their own way, in their own time. I mourned my sister's death sixteen years after it happened. When I was fifteen, I experienced the full gamut of emotions at the time of her death and afterwards, but not until I was coming to terms with another loss in my life did I truly feel the loss of my sister. When I contemplated what we never shared, and would never share, I was crushed.

I felt all my thoughts, emotions, hopes, and fears bombarding me as I grieved the end of my marriage in 1990. In trying to make the pieces of my life fit together, I found some pieces didn't fit. Much was lost. I learned what pressure was in the process, and I suffered.

I watched my two innocent sleeping children and knew I had to be strong. For them and for me. I felt so alone and at that moment my mind turned to Pina. She hadn't been in my thoughts for some time, and the dam that had been building up inside of me over the years finally burst. I felt her loss acutely, and I experienced such total anguish at my inability to articulate to her all my feelings, my regrets, my love. I decided to write her a letter to make things right; or, at least, attempt to do so:

November 28, 1991

Dear Pina,

I'm all stressed out and I wish you were here to help me in these trying times. I'm sorry we never got the chance to work out our adolescent immaturities and develop a strong sisterly bond. Life is such a struggle at times. I know a lot of people are far worse off than me, but I can't help feeling overwhelmed and exhausted. My spirit is low and I'm impatient and angry. I burst into tears at the slightest provocation. I'm worried because there's a heaviness in my chest and I feel that stress is taking over my life. All the demands of work, the kids, and the divorce are taking their toll on me.

It's go, go, go all the time, and I think it has come to the point where I've got to make changes or I will become sick. I just want peace to return to my life, and I want my kids to have an emotionally healthy childhood, in spite of the divorce.

You know, Pina, once when Sarah was a baby, her sleeping face seemed to be a vision of you. Maybe I had seen that expression on one of your baby pictures... I don't know. Could it be possible that there is a part of you in Sarah? I know one thing: she's artistic, like you were. Maybe what you and I never had as sisters, I'm supposed to have with Sarah...

I'm sorry if I ever hurt your feelings. I miss what we could have had. I know you would have been my friend. My only consolation is that you're in a better place, close to God.

Dear Pina, pray for all of us—me, my children Sarah and Jordan, our parents and brothers—that we can come to peace in our lives. I will say this prayer for you: Eternal rest grant upon Pina, oh Lord, and let perpetual light shine upon her. May she rest in peace. Amen.

I never told you, but I love you.

When I completed the letter, I was emotionally spent, but at peace. I had finally mourned my sister.

Cycles

"Sit here," I say gently, maternally, leading him to the bench in the foyer. "This way, so you won't lose your balance."

"Okay," he complies, and sits a little off to one side. He straightens and leans forward, reaching for the boots I have placed by his feet. He takes one and, after some pushing and straining, plants his right foot firmly in it and straightens again in his seat, aware that his nose is dripping. He reaches for the handkerchief in his pants pocket and dabs at his nose, then shoves it back into his pocket. He stands suddenly and looks alertly to one side, as if infused with sudden energy.

"Your other boot," I remind him, and he promptly sits down again. This boot gives him more trouble.

"Let me help you," I murmur, afraid of offending him in his fledgling efforts, yet hesitant to stand by and watch him struggle. While I am kneeling on the floor, I complete the task by pulling up both zippers of his boots. *Maybe I should have let him do it all by himself,*

I think. *Maybe I shouldn't step in so quickly. I'm always encouraging my junior kindergarten students to dress themselves.*

"It's nice out," I say brightly. "You won't have to wear your heavy coat." I hold out a medium jacket hanging on a rack, and he extends one arm and then the other. The zipper presents a problem. Again, I step in helpfully. *I'll just start him off,* I tell myself. *He'll be able to zip it up the rest of the way.* He does, and I feel content, satisfied at his ability.

"Here's your hat." I plop it on his head, but perhaps it's just a bit off-kilter, because he reaches to take it off and position it exactly where he wants it. I smile inwardly.

He puts on his gloves next. I'm not sure if all the fingers wind up in the right spots, but I'm not going to do a check unless he indicates they're uncomfortable.

"Grab your hankie—your nose is about to drip again," I tell him, looking down. He pulls off a mitt and plunges his hand into his pants pocket, but by the time he holds the hankie up, his nose has already dripped twice. He wipes it anyway.

When his mitt is back on, he takes a deep breath. I give him a pat of encouragement and think, *He's so trusting and innocent, like a baby bird waiting for its mother to feed it.*

I open the door and hold it for him as we step outside. It is unusually mild for an early February day at two degrees Celsius. The sun, though, is becoming bashful, sinking behind clumps of clouds and denying us its warming presence. I hope it doesn't stay cloudy.

When the sun disappears, a part of me disappears along with it, and I feel a cloud on my spirit.

A gust of wind picks up. We don't even take a dozen steps away from the house before he says to me, "Where are we going? It's too windy."

"Here, I'll lift the collar of your jacket. We'll just stay out for a few minutes; it's good to get some fresh air." He's had the flu and is more sensitive to the cold than I am.

I think at first that he might insist on going back inside, but he doesn't, and we start our walk. I lead the way, down the walkway, past the garden blanketed in snow to the gate, which leads to a back lane. To the west, the Inco superstack puffs away, its concrete body impervious to the sulfurous fumes it exhales.

Things have changed in this neighbourhood, I realize, and things have not. As we walk slowly through the brown, slushy snow in the lane, my gaze flits to the poles with hewn tips stacked in bunches in the corner of many yards, along with the occasional broken hockey stick that has been officially retired for garden use. For the beanstalks, of course. *Faggiolina* in our Calabrese dialect.

A yearly cycle. Hoeing, seeding, watering, tending, supporting the stalks with poles to allow their lanky foliage to climb upward. I used to love the way the plants intertwined around the poles, and I often wondered as a child how they ever managed by themselves in the past, with no poles or people to put them up. For as long as I can remember, I watched my parents sink the poles into the earth, satisfied when their work was done, and even more satisfied when the beans were ready to pick later in the summer, dangling in verdant profusion from their leafy stalks. I can almost smell the mixture of *faggiolina,* potatoes, and sometimes even zucchini, bubbling away in a mixture of olive oil, water, onions, a little tomato—with of course a sprig of fresh *basilico,* also from the garden, thrown in.

A yearly cycle, that's what it is. *Yes. Everything is a cycle. Life is a cycle. Parents have children. Children become parents. Parents have children. And so on. What a philosopher I am,* I mock myself, wryly. *The mistress of the obvious.*

We turn the corner, both silent, and approach the church. "Do you want to go this way?" I ask.

"Okay," he says. I help him across the street, averting a patch of ice, and we continue our slow, measured steps.

I wonder how long the church has had those stained-glass doors. I regard them thoughtfully. My glance drops to the swirling design of the interlocking brick path outside the church.

The wind picks up again and swirls around us, biting at our exposed skin. "Let's go home," he says, turning his head to avoid a gust. "It's too cold."

The sun is still playing hide-and-seek, ignoring our discomfort. "When it's sunny, it's warmer and nicer to walk," he explains. As if he must explain. Perhaps his eyes are more sensitive to the cold because of his recent eye surgery.

"At least we got a little exercise," I tell him.

We return home by the main street instead of the back lane. He seems so small beside me; I feel a rush of protectiveness as he shuffles forward.

Cycles, I find myself thinking. *We have to accept the cycles of life.*

We step inside the house, and I help with the ritual of undressing. The door leading to the basement is open, and I close it to allay my fear that he might stumble and fall.

I keep my coat on. "It's time for me to go home," I tell him, kissing him. "Bye, Dad. I'll see you soon." My mother appears from the kitchen to help him.

Cycles. Children become parents. Parents become children.

He lifts a hand that has planted many, many beanpoles. He waves it stiffly, the only way he can, having Parkinson's disease. With a hint of a smile, he turns to me and thanks me, and I gaze into his good eye, the eye that hasn't clouded over from glaucoma.

In it, I see the sun coming out.

Illumination

You've heard the saying: "It takes a martyr to live with a saint." Well, our Italian-Canadian heritage is replete with both martyrs and saints who made the trans-Atlantic journey with our immigrant parents, tucked away within the folds of their baggage. Even more concretely, within the folds of our parents' conscience, which carried, in no small measure, a cruet of Catholic guilt. The saints, whether they appeared on prayer cards or plates or even as statues, were displayed prominently in every home to bless and protect our immigrant family, to give our parents faith and hope as they started a new life in Canada.

As children we didn't always understand our parents' devotion or religious customs, but as the years passed, we gained a deeper appreciation of their time-honoured traditions.

The saints are with us from the moment we appear on this planet, for our parents have surely named us after one or more of their parents, who beheld the name of a favoured saint. So, your first name might very well be Lucia or Anna or Antonio or Pietro, most likely followed by the all-time favourite, Maria, or of course, Giuseppe. Blessed are those bearing the name of Jesus's parents!

As a first-generation Italian, born in Reggio Calabria and having immigrated to Canada at the age of three, I still felt the invisible yet iron pull of tradition when pondering the name of my daughter twenty-two years later. I decided against using the name of either one of her grandmothers, and chose Sarah simply because I liked it, not because of its biblical significance. However, I knew that I had to somehow include a second name that had familial and religious significance; therefore, I decided to go with the ever-popular Maria. Officially, of course, she was Sarah Marie—I liked the sound of it—but she was called *Sara Maria* by both sets of grandparents.

My mother was quite pleased. The tradition of including Maria in our daughters' names would continue. She had named me Rosanna Maria, and she was called Carmela Maria Assunta. Her mother, my Nonna, also was Maria.

When it came time to name my son three years later, I again chose a first name that I liked, Jordan, and it, too, had biblical significance. Difficulty arose when deciding upon a second name. I could go with either Nicholas, after my father Nicola, or Paul, after my father-in-law, and satisfy my family's desire for a holy namesake, but I was worried that whatever name I chose, the other grandparent might feel offended.

Being the sensitive person that I am, I decided to go with Jordan Paul Nicholas and make everyone happy. And then I thought, *Oh, well, I picked three names, what's one more?* So I added Domenic, for the simple reason that I felt I owed it to *San Domenico Savio*, the patron saint of pregnant women, to whom I had prayed, at my mother's urging when I had experienced some problems in the first trimester, for the delivery of a healthy child.

I had, in the past, occasionally teased my mother about her superstitious beliefs, to which she would reply that they were truths, not superstitions. She procured a well-worn cloth amulet with the face of St. Domenic Savio that she had worn around her neck for each of her four pregnancies and she declared that I should wear it as well, so that *San Domenico* would protect my unborn child.

I hid my skepticism and wore the amulet to appease my mother's fears, and I had to smile inwardly at her contentment at my acquiescence. Her contentment continued as I progressed through my second and third trimester with no further problems. When I delivered a healthy baby boy at the end of August, somehow I subconsciously knew that the right thing to do was to credit *San Domenico* for his saintly intervention and honour him by bestowing my son with his name.

Domenico was a name that my mother had also chosen for my brother, the first boy born after two girls. His full name is Antonio Domenico Pasquale: Antonio to honour one of my mother's favourite saints, Domenico to thank for bringing forth a healthy baby, and

Pasquale to show respect to my father's father, Nonno Pasquale. My mother's father was dead, so she didn't have to worry about offending him, and his name, Cosimo, would be the name chosen for the next son, who was born two years later.

Nonno Pasquale was quite the character, may he rest in peace. He is scowling in the only photo we have of him in my mother's living room, placed next to a picture of his wife, whom many considered a saint. Nonno Pasquale demanded much of his sons, who helped him maintain the family farm. He was nicknamed "Pasquale *u riccutu*" in our dialect, which hints at his prosperity (in land), but I have heard murmurings of his less-than-spendthrift nature.

As the story goes, when my mother gave birth to my brother, she and my father decided to call him Antonio Domenico Pasquale. That was his official name, but they called him Pasquale, probably to avoid a family conflict with Nonno Pasquale, who expected that the first boy would be named after him. You might think that such a matter would be inconsequential but let me assure you that family feuds in the south of Italy could be ignited with much less than the matter of name selection for a newborn. Once ignited, they could spread in such an incendiary fashion as to scorch many boughs of the family tree, in much the same way that a summer fire spreads its sizzling fingers over the dry, parched Calabrian countryside, inflaming the gnarled olive trees and ubiquitous oleanders and *fichi d'India*, what we know as prickly pears.

Apparently, Nonno Pasquale, who was reputedly prickly at the best of times, became inflamed when he heard through the local grapevine that my brother's *first* name was not officially Pasquale, it was *last.*

Madonna mia, I wish I could have been a fly in the town square that day! (Who knows, I might have been there, anyway, sitting on a relative's lap. I was two when my brother was born.)

I can just imagine Nonno Pasquale's omnipresent frown deepening at the news of my mother and father's deception, his more pronounced puffing of his pipe, of his rigid march into the *municipio* to demand inspection of the registry documents showing my brother's official name. The latter is not my imaginary musing; my mother attests to this.

I suppose that Nonno Pasquale was appeased eventually, since nobody dared call my brother anything but Pasquale... but I am positive this furor over my brother's name incited heartfelt prayers to a favourite saint or martyr for peace in the family from our more pious family members, as well as exasperation from the least pious, accompanied with muttered or even full-blown expletives.

Expletives in the Italian (and Italian-Canadian) tradition almost always involve the name of a saint, or a member of the Holy Family. You've heard them. You've been confused by some of them. Which one of us, while growing up, hasn't wondered at the logic of the curse *Porco Dio? Pig God? Pig God!* (God forgive me for committing these blasphemous utterances to paper!)

And then when we heard *porco cane*, that made no sense either. Pig dog! Was it perhaps the aspiration of the P in conjunction with the double hard C sound that somehow helped release some of the frustration that was trapped inside the curser's body, and had to be expelled with such vociferous force? *Madonna!*

Expletives aside, the saints and martyrs have a sacred place in every Italian-Canadian home, and you were made aware of the importance of religion and saints in the family from infancy. You were gifted gold medallions bearing the image of the Virgin Mary or Jesus when you were baptized. And when you received First Communion. And when you were confirmed. When you were married, you received a very large, framed picture of the Holy Family that you were advised to place over your marital bed. Every Sacrament was accompanied by a medallion, statue, or painting of a saint. When *your* children were baptized, your parents gifted them with gold medallions, and the rituals began anew.

The only "Group of Seven" paintings you had hanging in your home were the illustrations and paintings of Jesus as a curly-haired baby in a manger, Jesus in the arms of St. Anthony, Jesus praying in the garden of Gethsemane, Jesus on the cross, Mary holding Jesus, Jesus lying on Mary *(La Pietà)*, and Jesus rising from the dead. *Jesus!*

Your kitchen had a copy of Leonardo da Vinci's "The Last Supper" on the wall. Your dining room had a bigger version on its wall. Your living room had a picture or statue of any number of saints—this depended on the patron saint of your parents' village back home, which your parents felt compelled to venerate in their newly adopted country. *San Nicola di Bari*—St. Nicholas of Bari—was *our* Saint, the patron saint of our village of Camini. Above every doorway and/or on other walls, there was either a wooden crucifix, or a plate or picture bearing the image of the Madonna or a martyr in various states of agony: A crown of spiky thorns above a blood-tinged forehead; dolorous eyes on a plate held by sad *Santa Lucia*, patron saint of sight, vision, and wisdom, herself missing her eyeballs; *Santo Rocco*, patron saint of dogs and the falsely accused, among others, watching the open sores on his leg being licked by dogs. It's a wonder you didn't have recurring nightmares. Or maybe you did. Perhaps some of you are still in therapy.

Alongside a holy picture or plate was affixed the yearly palm creation, fashioned out of fresh palm leaves distributed on Palm Sunday. Your mother made crosses or tiny hearts out of the strips of palm and gave them to each member of the family to hang in their room, or in the car for protection.

When my mother was in her seventies, she had a serious heart attack. I visited daily and my siblings and I took turns staying with her overnight once she was released from the hospital. I slept in the room that used to belong to my parents. The first night I spent in there, I looked at all the pictures and statues collected over the years: the Holy Family above the bed; the statue of St. Joseph that I brought back from my Grade 11 school trip to St. Joseph's Oratory in Montreal, Quebec; the framed picture that my sister brought back from her Grade 7 trip to the Martyrs' Shrine in Midland, Ontario; the statue of the Madonna among pink flowers that I gave my mother when she had her gallbladder operation in 1982; the plate of Pope John Paul II given as a Christmas gift to my mother by one of my children.

In the top drawer of one night table, there were dozens of holy pictures and prayer booklets from the old country, along with some missal books from St. Anthony's, my mother's church—and my childhood neighbourhood church—only steps away from her house. My mother slept in the room next to this one, and she kept Italian prayer cards of St. Anthony and St. Nicholas by her bedside.

When it was my turn to stay with her during the night, I'd spend some time in Ma's room watching the Food Network—she'd gotten me hooked on *Iron Chef America*—or an Italian program, and then I'd retire to my room. I'd turn off the lights and ponder many things: the sacrifices my parents made to leave the old country and settle in Canada with four young children; the hardships they had to endure, adjusting to a new language and culture; the challenge of raising their children to be proud Canadians while never forgetting their mother Italia; and finally, how lucky I was to have been blessed with two identities, although sometimes it seemed like such a struggle while growing up.

In the dark room, I felt illuminated...

I looked up at the wall above me and realized with a start that the crucifix hanging below the picture of the Holy Family was glowing.

A glow-in-the-dark Jesus.

I smiled.

I had seen the light.

Daddy's Girl

I am staring Death in the eye at the dawning of a new millennium. It is staring back at me unflinchingly with its metallic gaze, all the while hovering over the inert body it is embracing. Inside the person it has embraced, it is wreaking silent havoc, squeezing the life out of its victim's heart, smothering its palpitations, impervious to the emergency doctor's earlier heart-thumping techniques.

Death's fingers caress its victim's limbs, leaving blue-black imprints from the feet to the neck that resemble a storm-mottled sky. They say that eyes are the mirror of the soul: the victim's eyes are open in a face bloated under an oxygen mask. But the patient's soul is indiscernible, his eyes impenetrable. The metallic gaze is not a figment of my literary imagination; there is an actual metallic-blue plate that has slid over one cornea like a galactic shield.

He's having a heart attack right now, the doctor says.

Is having. Not had. Is having. Now. Still.

Right now, I repeat numbly, tasting Death's imminence, all the while squeezing the patent's hand. My father's hand.

My own heart constricts as I listen to the doctor's explanations of the results of some tests. Can I get a priest? I ask. My Catholic upbringing tells me this must be done for the sake of the patient who cannot advocate for himself.

A priest arrives shortly after, murmurs the appropriate prayers for the family, then leaves. My family members take turns being with their loved one—*my* loved one—each uttering words of encouragement, words of love. I bide my time in the congested waiting area, realizing that I have to be prepared to face the ultimate outcome.

I think it out, breathing rhythmically to stay relaxed. If it's my father's time to die, then he will be at peace, having suffered declining health the past several years due to the insidious progression of Parkinson's disease. If it is life, then we will face the challenges as they come.

The reality is your father has a ten per cent chance of pulling through... We listen to the specialist's words a few hours later, on the first day of the year 2000. The Y2K anxiety of the past weeks has gone, only to be replaced by anxiety about my father's chances of survival.

But my father beats the odds. He's still alive after a week. He begins to show more signs of life... He pulls out his intravenous tubes. But he still needs complete care. I take the lunch shift so my mother can go home and rest. I am left with the task of feeding my father his puréed lunch.

I proceed with a heavy heart, restraining my tears, encouraging him with words I used on my infant children years ago. Open wide now. You need to eat so you can get strong. Peas are good for you.

My father is like a newborn, helpless. He can't walk, he can't feed himself, and he can't talk. All speech seems to have been suspended, locked inside. I listen to myself having a one-way conversation. I talk about anything, everything. The slightest inclination of his head is sometimes the only indication I have that he has understood what I have said.

Perhaps he will never regain his speech, I think.

He proves me wrong.

His voice is raspy, incomprehensible at times, but the words begin to come. As the days pass, my conversations are no longer completely one-sided. My father tells me about the pigeons he saw. He asks me if I want a peach or a pear. He inquires about the sausages hanging as they cure. He talks about his father as if he were still alive. He believes he is in the old country. He waves to a friend who isn't there.

I wonder if his vision has deteriorated further. He has been diagnosed with glaucoma. I ask him if he likes my new jacket. He says he does. I ask him what colour it is. He says black. My jacket is red. My heart bleeds.

Much of the colour has gone from his life, I realize. He is fading, himself, like a photograph exposed to too much sunlight; but unlike a photograph, he cannot be restored.

Tears blur my vision. My inner vision clicks on, highlighting a lifetime of unforgettable moments with him: my father comforting me after a bad dream; helping me with Grade 5 math; buying me, to my elation, a huge blackboard for my eleventh birthday and getting my younger brothers to play school with me. My father in his garden, raising rabbits and chickens. I hear him laughing at the antics of my newborn daughter and holding my newborn son three years later. My father at the specialist's office the same year, learning he has Parkinson's disease. My father becoming stiffer as his illness progresses, crying when I rub his aching back with liniment yet doing the *Tai Chi for Parkinson's* video exercises with me.

My father squeezing my hand in the emergency room, his heart in crisis.

My father.

I let my tears flow freely as I stand at his bedside, wondering how much more life there is in him. I feel so powerless.

Visiting hours are over. I squeeze his hand gently, murmuring I love you directly in his ear. I wait. He squeezes my hand more tightly than usual.

Without opening his eyes, he utters a muffled reply. I love you, too.

I'll come back tomorrow, I tell him. Sweet dreams.

As I leave the hospital, I realize the only power I have is to pray that my father is blessed with good dreams tonight.

In brilliant colour.

Learning My Lesson

I had just received my first long-term teaching assignment days earlier. It was November, and a teacher in an inner-city school had to take an early maternity leave. I was offered the position teaching Core French and Art to Grades 7 and 8 students, and I was warned it would be a tough assignment. I knew it was in a "rough" part of town. But I was fresh out of teacher's college, full of enthusiasm, and all of twenty-one. I accepted.

I had four classes with over a hundred students in total to deal with. Some were friendly, and some were quiet and observant, but it seemed that most of the students were loud and disrespectful. All my wonderful lesson plans seemed to go awry as discipline became my number one priority. My head spun as I tried to identify the "class clowns" with their inappropriate language, snickering, and rude body noises. I'm sure it was a foregone conclusion to some of them—a challenge to bring the new teacher down. I felt they had succeeded at one point, when I found myself weeping in the principal's office, telling her that I couldn't take it anymore.

The principal, a Catholic nun, was very supportive and marched into the classroom, ready to issue suspensions. I was simply to tell her who the culprits were. The class settled down and she left, advising me to send her anyone who was being disrespectful.

I began reviewing French vocabulary and was asking simple questions relating to Christmas. "What will you give your mother for Christmas?" My eyes scanned the classroom. Several students, the ones who had never given me any trouble, had their hands up. Others had bored looks and were doodling in their notebooks. Others simply had their heads down. I decided to single out one of the heads-down group. I'll call him Robert here.

"*Robert, qu'est-ce que tu vas donner à ta mère pour Noël?*"

The students with their heads down looked up. The others stopped doodling and stared at me. *Progress*, I thought with satisfaction. I finally had their undivided attention. I turned to Robert.

Robert had looked up, but his face, unlike the others, had contorted into a mask of pain. "I hate you!" he cried, then ran from the room.

What had I done? Stunned, I met the sea of frozen, unbelieving faces in the room.

"His mother committed suicide, Miss," one of the girls near me said softly.

I wanted to cry. "I didn't know," I murmured in shock. "I didn't know."

Why, of all the students in the class, did I have to call on Robert? If I had known about his mother, I would never have used that question as an example. I felt heartbroken and battered, crushed and alone. *Poor Robert*, I wept inwardly. *How must he be feeling?*

The next few moments were a blur. Robert ran to the principal's office, and she brought him back just outside the classroom, allowing me to approach him. His body was slumped in sorrow. I did the only thing I could do: I spoke to him with my heart. I told him how sorry I was, that I hadn't known what had happened, and that I would never have wanted to hurt him or anybody in that way. I asked him for forgiveness.

Over the years, I have learned that people listen when you speak from the heart. Robert believed me. I think he saw his pain reflected in my eyes. He sensed my sincerity and genuine sorrow. Robert taught me that you can't assume that everyone in your class has a mother and father, that you should find out as much as you can about the students you will have in your care. Like everybody else, students have histories that may be filled with pain and loss, and you must remember you are not teaching "subjects" but human beings with feelings and vulnerabilities.

As I struggled with the challenges and the shifting personalities of many students that first year, I realized that teaching was always going to be a learning and shifting experience, full of successes and mistakes, triumphs and tribulations. Lessons to teach and lessons to learn.

Robert gave me my first gift as a teacher: the gift of forgiveness. And a lesson I'll never forget.

Nonna's Legacy

I can hardly remember this tiny, black-garbed woman without a rosary in her hand. *My Nonna.*

For most of my life, my maternal grandmother lived an entire continent away. I spent only a brief period of time in her company during her ninety-three years, which came to a peaceful end in 1991: the first three years after I was born—before we moved to Canada—and when I returned to visit as a child for six months with my family, then later as a teenager for two months in the summer of 1974. In 1982, Nonna waived a longstanding resolution and, at eighty-four years of age, summoned the courage to leave our native Italy to come visit us for a month in Sudbury, Ontario.

I relied on my parents to furnish details of my infant years living with Nonna Maria, and these, along with other shared accounts of her life, have enriched my own impressions of her.

Nonna was totally devoted to her faith. It must have been this unwavering faith that helped her to surmount the many challenges and hardships she faced over the years. She was born Maria Bombardieri in 1898 in Gioiosa Ionica, Calabria. The last decades of the 19th century were not easy ones for the mostly agrarian populations of the South. After Italy's unification in 1861, Calabria was one of the territories that suffered from the excessive tax incentives of the new liberal government. This caused increased poverty, rebellion, and disillusionment for the landless peasants who had hoped that unification would bring, as General Giuseppe Garibaldi had promised, land reforms that would allow them a portion of land to own, cultivate, and keep their families fed. The coastal populations also had to deal with the rising incidents of malaria.

In 1921, at twenty-three years of age, Nonna Maria married Cosimo Adavastro, a handsome young man from the nearby village of Camini. One of the six children they had died shortly after birth. Then Cosimo had fought in WWI, and the story that has been passed down is that shrapnel from a bullet during battle eventually caused his early death after their ten years of marriage. What stamina and courage it must have taken for Nonna Maria at thirty-three years of age to raise five children alone, the youngest—my mother—being only one month old.

With a small pension endowed to her by the Italian government, Nonna Maria managed a little shop in Camini—the *tabacchino* in our Calabrian dialect—which provided all kinds of cheeses, salami, nuts, and household items, including salt and tobacco, *sale e tabacchi.* At night she sewed for her own family and for other people in the village, who paid her in flour, grain, oil, fruits, and vegetables. On her way to and from the cemetery where Nonno Cosimo was buried, Nonna Maria would inevitably fill a basket with prickly pears from bushes growing wild on the hillsides, and with herbs like wild fennel and chicory.

Life was hard: my mother's stories attested to the constant struggle. When I was young and had the audacity to leave the crusts from my sandwich on my plate, my mother would admonish me for wasting food. "If you had been brought up during the war," she'd start, and go on to describe my Nonna's efforts to keep them all fed.

Along with the daily challenge of working and raising five children—three of them active boys—Nonna Maria's strength was further tested in 1944 with the death of her eighteen-year-old daughter, Anna Rosa, whose passing is still shrouded in mystery.

The tiny village of Camini was far from more advanced medical centres, and nearby doctors hadn't been able to diagnose Anna Rosa's ailment. My mother, who was thirteen at the time of her sister's death, recalls that Anna Rosa had no fever, and maintains that her golden-haired sister succumbed to depression and died of a broken heart, caused by the knowledge that the man to whom she had promised her undying love had been, through his family's intervention, promised to another while he was away at war.

While Anna Rosa lay ill, the mother of this man paid her a visit and gifted her with a clock. It was *mala fortuna,* my mother said, bad luck which signalled Anna Rosa's final days with its ominous ticking.

She died just days afterwards.

Compounding Nonna Maria's grief was the fact that two of her eldest sons, Francesco and Giuseppe, were fighting in World War II, the younger of whom had been captured with his squadron by the Germans. As a mother myself, I can only imagine the incessant anguish and despair, knowing your child was a prisoner of war. It was much later that Nonna Maria received the news that eighteen-year-old Giuseppe had closely escaped execution when the Nazis were defeated. My mother recalled the exact words on the postcard sent by one of Giuseppe's compatriots from Messina, Sicily: *Ritornando della Germania. Lasciai in buona salute il vostro famigliare, che presto farà ritorno.* "Returning from Germany. I left your family member in good health, and he will be returning soon," it read.

"*Grazie a Dio!*" Nonna cried, weeping at the good news that her prayers and faith in God for her son's salvation had been answered. To demonstrate her gratitude, she joined a procession of other villagers who were either praying for their sons and husbands away at war, or thanking God for having received special graces, such as their loved ones' safe return home. Nonna Maria woke up at 3:00 a.m. every day for a week to make the three-hour procession up into the mountains, to arrive at an underground cave containing the shrine of the *Madonna di Montestella.* After prayers of praise and gratitude, the group headed back to Camini.

Such an act of faith was commonplace in the lives of many villagers; the early morning journeys along dark, perilous mountain paths to their sacred destination still leaves me in awe. Such courage, focus, and energy! Regardless of your religious perspective and beliefs, you cannot deny the communal support and inner strength engendered by such selfless actions.

Months after the initial news of Giuseppe's imminent return, Nonna Maria was elated by the return of her eldest son Francesco and later of young Giuseppe, just two days before the first anniversary of Anna Rosa's death. Giuseppe's war memories would haunt him for years.

At the time, nothing seemed more important than celebrating such a momentous occasion. Nonna Maria set about preparing a feast including pigeon soup, rabbit, and pasta dishes, while her brother-in-law ensconced himself in the doorway on one side of the narrow street—*Via Alberto*—offering each passerby a drink from the demijohn of red wine positioned next to him. I can just imagine the scene as I recall Nonna's house from my two visits: family members and *paesani* laughing and hugging, kissing and crying, lifting their glasses of wine and exclaiming *Salute!* with an even deeper appreciation of the meaning of life and health than ever before. And Nonna Maria's black eyes glistening with tears at the long-awaited reunion with her sons, her voice raised along with her glass. "*Grazie a Dio!*" Thanks be to God.

I can imagine the feast she prepared with her exceptional culinary skills honed over the years. Even during recent visits to my hometown of Camini, Nonna Maria's reputation as an amazing cook lived on. Her spaghetti sauce and meatballs, stuffed eggplant, and countless other dishes were prepared to my mother's exacting taste after we immigrated to Canada, and I am proud to say that I have continued delighting my family with these traditional Calabrian meals.

To further demonstrate Nonna's gratitude for God's grace in bringing her sons home safely from war, she pledged to refrain from eating meat for two additional days of the week: Wednesday and Saturday. She was already abstaining from eating meat on Fridays. Even during her visit to Canada in 1982, Nonna Maria insisted that my mother honour her pledge, and vociferously scolded her once or twice for trying to pass off stuffed peppers as meatless when indeed they were not.

Nonna Maria, like the other villagers in Camini, participated in age-old Calabrian traditions that combined Christian and pagan practices. She strongly believed in truths that subsequent generations dismissed as mere superstitions. I recall her sudden alarm when, as a teenager, I took her black kerchief and tied it around my head to see how it would look. Every woman wore a kerchief to church, and I wanted to wear one too. I was shocked when Nonna Maria whipped it off my head and made the sign of the cross, scolding me for inviting *mala fortuna*—bad luck—into the family. She warned me of other evils that would befall us if we placed a black article of clothing on the bed, or if we spilled oil. It amazed me when my mother voiced some of the same beliefs, proving how beliefs and traditions can become rooted from one generation to the next, and how not even modern science, with its astounding revelations, can change some of these ancient beliefs.

Nonna Maria was a tiny woman: under five feet tall with silver hair reaching down to the small of her back. She kept her hair hidden, revealing it only at night when she combed it out before going to bed, or early in the morning when she braided it into a tight bun. From the time her husband Cosimo died, she insisted on wearing a black shirt and skirt which reached to her ankles. She carried her grief stoically throughout the years, visiting his grave daily, and raising five children while enduring further pain with the loss of her beloved daughter, Anna Rosa, after whom I am named.

Another event that highlights this woman's incredible courage is her insistence on being present at the removal of her husband's bones from his grave some twenty years after his death—a common practice to make room in the overcrowded cemetery. The bones would then be placed in an ossuary. Nonna Maria witnessed and even helped remove the bones of Nonno Cosimo, returning home with her face "yellow as a lemon," my mother recalled.

As the years went by, Nonna Maria's faith and dedication to her family was ever-present. She showed her love in her cooking, and she used her amazing crocheting talents to create a bedspread for my mother and one for each of her seven granddaughters, all while reciting the rosary, sometimes silently, sometimes aloud with her grandchildren. I remember reciting the words with her: *Ave Maria, piena di grazia...*

You must see one of her bedspreads to appreciate all the work and time involved. It is a gift I will always treasure.

Living with or close to your grandmother is sure to leave some kind of impression on your life. I lived without my Nonna for most of my life, yet her life and example have touched me deeply. Whenever I feel the pressures of my life start to overwhelm me, I think of Nonna Maria's hardships and her unwavering faith in surmounting them. I hope that I, like my Nonna, will leave an indelible impression on my children and grandchildren, and that my example of living today will be a legacy for my grandchildren to treasure in the future.

Thanks, Nonna Maria. *Grazie di cuore.*

Time To Say Goodbye

His eyes are partially closed when I arrive. I approach the bed, wondering if I should just leave him be; perhaps he needs to sleep, perhaps he didn't sleep much during the night. He starts, as the shadow thrown by my body snuffs out the light entering the slit in his eyes. His eyelids flutter and a muffled greeting forms in his throat but never leaves his mouth.

His left hand lifts ever so slightly. It is an artist's palette, splattered with bruises of magenta and vermilion-tinged brown, puddles of eggplant purple and yellow-green. His fingers, swollen and pale, resemble a giant paw, and his wrist, dotted with the puncture marks from previous intravenous needles, is a freeway of veins. There is an IV attached even now, carrying precious potassium to his deprived body.

His muffled warbling continues, and his eyes begin to open. I lean forward, trying to ascertain their clarity, almost as if I expect the nebulous depths to dissipate just for me, so I can find the treasures that I know exist there. *Open, sesame!* Come on, a little more, that's it. His eyelashes rise and fall and then hold steady. I peer closely and only see the treasures that cataracts and glaucoma bring—murky opal stones with no fire.

Hey Dad, how are you doing?

I bend to kiss him on the cheek, and he moves his head slightly, a short jerk. I take it as a sign of recognition; he may not know who I am, but my voice is familiar.

It's me, Dad. I came to spend some time with you... Here, let me take your hand. It's so dry, just like mine. Why don't I put some cream on it? This hospital cream isn't bad; I'll just massage it on your skin. There... isn't that better? Now let me do your other hand.

Hey Dad, I saw a rabbit yesterday in my yard. It's so nice living out in the country. You get to see all kinds of wild animals. Let's see, what have we spotted in the forest... bears, two deer, a moose with her calf, and a fox. Do you remember when you used to go hunting in the old country, Dad? With your dog, Argo.

Is that a flicker of a nod? Does he understand my monologue? I have become used to half-hour-long soliloquies; he cannot respond, what with a nasal gastric tube that has been inserted in his nose and down his throat to carry liquid food to his stomach.

Maybe I shouldn't be talking about food when he lacks the power to control the mechanisms involved in one of the greatest of all pleasures: eating.

His swallowing processes no longer function. Eating out of a spoon puts him at a high risk for aspiration, the speech pathologist has determined after performing a swallowing assessment. The cause is most likely a combination of factors, she explains kindly: the advanced stage of Parkinson's disease, the heart attack he suffered two years earlier, and the small stroke that went undetected.

I'm afraid we'll eventually lose the battle, Dad's doctor has informed us at a family conference. His body is quitting on him. Your dad doesn't want a tube in his nose—he has pulled it out, which is why we have no choice but to restrain his arms. We're keeping him alive by mechanical means, but even what he is getting will not be able to sustain him forever. His condition is palliative.

I look at those cloth restraints now, holding my dad's wrists securely by his side, strapped around the metal frame of the bed.

Hey, Dad, your hands are cool; let me pull up this blanket. It's getting cooler outside. Mom wants me to pluck the rest of the tomatoes off the vines, so they don't freeze tonight. Imagine, Dad, it's only the beginning of September, and the forecast says it could go down to four below zero. You know Mom, eh, Dad? How she curses Christopher Columbus every time it gets too cold, because if he hadn't discovered America, we would have never left Italy, where it never freezes in September.

I wish I could remember the voyage. I know I was only three, and Mom told me the name of the ship was *Saturnia*, and that I was the only one in our family who didn't get seasick. I love the sea. If I could, I'd go back to Italy every summer.

It's funny to think of all the silly things that caused us angst growing up, eh, Dad? Do you remember in 1970 when bell-bottom pants were in style? I begged Mom to get me some, or even make them for me, so I could be like the rest of the kids in my Grade 5 class, and she told me I'd have to ask you when you got home from work. I spent a couple of hours worrying about whether you would consent or not... and you did!

I know you wanted to make your children happy, Dad, and when you and Mom were starting to get on your feet, and you bought your first house in 1969 for twenty-two thousand dollars, we felt like we were rich. Not arrogant rich, but the feeling of being rich enough to have our own house instead of renting. I think we could sense your pride, Dad, to have been able to find a house with an apartment on the top floor you could rent out to help with the mortgage, a backyard big enough to make a decent garden, and a detached garage—a shack, really—but it served its purpose, even housing chickens and rabbits for a while.

And you and Mom finally had your own room. I shared a brightly-painted pink room with Pina, and the two boys shared—what else—a blue room. I'll never forget the colour of the living room and kitchen when we bought the house, lime green and purple. Well, it was 1969 after all; psychedelic colours were popular back then.

Mom wanted the house freshly painted, remember, all neutral colours except for the pink and blue bedrooms. We had a lot of happy times in that house, eh, Dad? The birthdays, the Christmas and the Easter celebrations, the Confirmations, the weddings, the wine making.

Sad times, too, though...

You lost your eldest daughter, Pina, while we were still at that house, and I lost my sister. The spring of 1975. I'll never forget that dismal, rainy day, coming home from high school and hearing the news. Even now that I'm a parent, I can only imagine the pain you and Mom must have felt, losing a child on the brink of young adulthood from blood poisoning caused by a ruptured appendix. In this day and age, too.

You know, Dad, we never talked about it before. After all, I was only fifteen at the time, and she was seventeen—but I remember how dark life was for a while, no smiles for all those months, no laughter, no parties, no television. But eventually the smiles returned; I remember cheering inwardly for the return of your spirit, yours and Mom's, and the discarding of all the black mourning clothes. I do realize that mourning for a loved one may subside, but it doesn't ever really go away.

I was relieved that you and Mom could find some measure of happiness again, and I can't tell you the joy I felt a decade later, watching you with your first grandchild, my Sarah.

Hey, Dad, you're tired; your eyes are closing. I'm going to let you have a rest now. I'll come back soon, and we'll spend some more time together. Next time I'll bring my portable CD player so you can hear some nice Italian music. How about Andrea Bocelli? What a beautiful voice he has!

Good night, Dad, let me give you a kiss. I love you, you hear? *Ti voglio tanto bene.*

Will my father make it through the night? As I gaze with misty eyes on his curved, still figure, the words of one of my favourite Andrea Bocelli songs, "Time to Say Goodbye," resound in my head:

Con te partirò
Su navi per mari
Che, io lo so
No, no, non esistono più
Con te io li rivivrò
Con te partirò
Io con te

I'll go with you
on ships across seas
which... exist no longer;
with you I shall experience them again.
I'll go with you, I with you.

As I leave my father, my eyes spill salty tears from a sea of memories. *Arrivederci, Papà.*

Teshaylia The Blue

In September 2003, I was told that one of my kindergarten students had lost her mother to cancer during the summer. I reassured her father that I would watch her closely and help her in any way I could.

Little Teshaylia—what a lovely name!—was very quiet and subdued. I wanted to find a way to lift the sadness from her face. She didn't smile or laugh, not even when the rest of the class found me funny or silly. One day, as the children were sitting on the mat for Circle Time, Teshaylia suddenly stood up and came to me.

"Mrs. B., I miss my Mommy."

I looked at her sad blue eyes and hugged her, my heart breaking with the knowledge that she was missing her mother's loving arms. "I know, sweetheart," I murmured, feeling helpless.

I realized that I had to provide Teshaylia with a physical expression for the loss she was experiencing. At the colouring centre, she sometimes wrote her mother's name on a piece of paper and drew hearts beside it. Suddenly, I had an idea. I asked Teshaylia if she wanted to write a letter to her mom. She nodded and I transcribed the words she wanted to say: *Dear Mommy, I love you. I miss you.* Or: *Dear God, please take good care of my Mommy in heaven.* Teshaylia loved the colour blue and always picked blue stickers to add to her letters. She also liked to wear blue clothes. I nicknamed her "Teshaylia the Blue."

I brought Teshaylia a gift bag from home with angel faces on both sides, and I encouraged her to keep all her letters to her mom inside the angel bag, since her mother was an angel in heaven. Teshaylia created many letters over the weeks and months ahead, and I was happy to see that the preoccupied, quiet little girl I met in September was smiling often and even laughing.

My memories of Teshaylia fill me with emotion and gratitude for teaching me what teaching is all about. We are all vulnerable human beings, and we can make a difference in this world, helping each other through times of loss and grief.

One child at a time. And with God's help.

I wrote this poem at the end of the year, and gave it to Teshaylia's father:

Teshaylia the Blue

This is the story of a girl I knew;
the name of this girl was Teshaylia the Blue

Her eyes were blue waves of a shimmering sea,
that held a twinkle or two when she looked at me.

She had a sprinkling of freckles on her pretty face,
with a halo of hair that danced all over the place.

On the first day of school in 2003,
I said "Hello, little friends! I'm Mrs. B!"

She looked up at me from her place on the mat;
on either side of her, the twin sisters sat.

They really didn't know what to make of me,
their new kindergarten teacher, called Mrs. B.

Some children cried and didn't want to stay;
others were happy and just wanted to play.

Teshaylia looked around; she didn't cry,
but her eyes were sad, like grey clouds in the sky.

With eyes downcast and lashes long,
she looked as lost as a newborn fawn.

At circle time, she didn't raise her hand;
she seemed to be in a faraway land...

Perhaps in a place where unicorns roam,
prancing about in a sea of foam.

Perhaps in a secret fairy ring,
where elves and pixies like to sing.

Or maybe on a rainbow lighting the sky
with lollipop colours—a feast for the eye.

Finally, one day, she jumped up from the mat,
as light and as limber as a calico cat.

She came up to me, and I drew her near.
"I miss my Mommy," she said in my ear.

What could I tell her to help ease the pain?
How could I make her eyes sparkle again?

"Your Mom's an angel," I said, "in heaven above.
And like all angels, she's surrounded by love.

She is gone from this earth, but you will find,
she still lives in your heart and in your mind.

When you think of her, she is thinking of you,
my little Teshaylia, Teshaylia the Blue."

I saw her eyes flicker; had she understood at all?
How could I explain something so big to someone so small?

"Mrs. B., is it snack time?" a boy named Callum called out.
"My stomach is grumbling," added Blake with a shout.

"Let's have something to eat," I announced with a smile.
Hugging Teshaylia, I said, "We'll talk more in a while."

After snack time, the children went to centres to play;
Teshaylia was at the writing centre, where I quickly made my way.

She had coloured a heart a brilliant blue,
with the word "Mommy" beside it and "I love you."

"Do you want to write Mom a letter?" I said and pulled up a chair.
She stopped and she gave me a wide-eyed stare.

Suddenly she smiled, then grinned from ear to ear.
I smiled back; I wanted to cheer.

I asked Teshaylia what she wanted to say;
I would help her write down her words that way.

"I love you, Mommy. I miss you," she wrote,
drawing hugs and kisses to end the note.

Then she decorated the page with a picture or two,
using her favourite colour—a brilliant blue.

The days went by, autumn leaves danced bright.
Squirrels prepared for winter, the Canada geese took flight.

Teshaylia kept writing and colouring too;
writing to Mom was her favourite thing to do.

I gave her a special bag with angels on either side,
to hold every letter she made with so much pride.

It made her happy; it was a special way,
to bring her close to her Mommy, day after day.

As the winter wind blew and snow covered the ground,
sad little Teshaylia could no longer be found.

In her place was a girl with bright, happy eyes,
that shone like stars in the heavenly skies.

At last the snow melted; robins began to appear,
their cheerful song announcing, "Spring is here!"

New life began as the sun warmed the land,
a tender caress from God's loving hand.

As if He wanted to say, to everybody on earth:
"Don't forget: I am with you from the day of your birth."

As Teshaylia played outside one lovely spring day,
I'm sure the warm breeze carried God's message her way:

"Don't worry, my little Teshaylia the Blue.
Mommy's safe here with me, and we're always near you.

Love never dies; believe me, it's true.
Like the sun, moon and stars, our love shines for you."

To my dear Teshaylia... with love from Mrs. B.

Bears And Good News

When I first discovered in September 2005 that one of the students in my Junior Kindergarten class had leukemia, my heart sank.

His name was Jordan, and he had previously been diagnosed at a mere eighteen months. He had completed a series of chemotherapy sessions at the Hospital for Sick Children ("Sick Kids") in Toronto, and as he was in remission, his doctor had said that he could begin school.

I met Jordan and his mother, Shannon, on the first day of school. Jordan looked the picture of health, with beautiful blue eyes and angelic features. Jordan loved my silly jokes and laughed often. By the end of the day, he was tired, as many of the children were, but as the days and weeks went by, I noticed that it was Jordan who often nodded off while sitting propped against the wall to wait for the bus at the end of the day.

When school started up again after the Christmas break, Jordan was absent. Did he have a cold? The flu? I prayed that it was something minor, and then I received the devastating news that he had suffered a relapse of leukemia and that he was back at Sick Kids.

The previous week, Jordan had complained of a headache and problems with his left eye. He could not see anything out of it. Shannon arranged for urgent consultation. Tests revealed that the fluid around Jordan's spinal column and brain were full of cancer cells.

When I heard the news that Jordan was back in treatment, I was overwhelmed with feelings of anxiety and worry. I became sadder with every negative thought: *Jordan may not get through this... This is too much for a four-year-old to survive.* I masked my sadness while teaching, but my heart was always heavy.

I suddenly realized one day that my faith was lagging. I *had* to change my perspective. *Jordan will beat this. Jordan will get stronger and survive. Jordan will come back home.* I would channel my thoughts with these affirmations, and I would not let negative thoughts poison my thinking any longer.

I immediately thought of Norman, a student I had taught in my Grade 8 class twenty years earlier. Norm had beaten childhood leukemia, and just recently I heard that he'd gotten married.

I was jubilant. From now on, I told myself, I would think of Norm whenever I thought of Jordan. Norm had been strong enough to survive childhood leukemia, and so would Jordan!

With these positive thoughts, I drove to a store that I knew had some plush toys. I wanted to send one to Jordan, to let him know that I was thinking about him. What I found literally took my breath away.

The store had just received a new line of plush bears. There were girl bears and boy bears. I picked up one of the latter and then realized that each bear had a specific name sewn into it, and under the name, there was a characteristic that described the bear.

I stood frozen, looking down at the bear I had chosen. His name was... NORMAN. And below it, the word "Strong."

I don't know how long I stood there, but I was completely stunned. Just *moments* after I had thought about Norm, *this* had happened. It was incredible. NORMAN. Strong.

I read the little booklet that was attached to the bear. There was no question. This bear was mine. This bear was going to be Jordan's.

I rushed home. I re-read the information. This bear was from a line called THE GOOD NEWS BEARS™, a creation of illustrator and designer, Amy Wulfing. One page of the tiny booklet read: "Each one of us, the 'Good News' bears... Reminders of God's love and care; God's Word and a special prayer. A friend to hold, a heart to share..."

And on another page: "THE GOOD NEWS BEARS 'bear witness' to God's precious gift of love. The scripture verse and prayers that they carry remind us of God's presence (and presents!) in our everyday moments. May God's Word encourage, and inspire, give hope and comfort, and bless your heart with His amazing love."

Continued on another side: "THE GOOD NEWS BEARS... Bearing the Good News of Jesus 'for such a time as this!'"

I looked again at the butterscotch bear with his black eyes and nose. On his chest was a red heart with black stitching around it, and a cross stitched inside. He wore a hooded grey pullover with a front pouch and pockets. Then I read the scripture passage on the card bearing his name. Under "NORMAN" and "Strong" were the words from Psalm 28:7: "The Lord is my strength and my shield; My heart trusts in Him, and I am helped."

And below that, a prayer: "Dear Jesus, it's not always easy to do the right things, sometimes I get tired, and discouraged, and want to give up. Please help me to be strong and keep me safe. Amen." (From Galatians 6 and Psalm 59:9, NAS).

At this point, tears were streaming down my face. I had needed to hear those words at that moment, and I hoped those words would be a source of strength and hope for Jordan's parents. I proceeded to wrap up the bear, and I sent it to Sick Kids the very next day by express post, still overcome by the fact that I had picked up a bear named NORMAN first, and not a BENJAMIN or an ABIGAIL.

When Shannon received the package, she was very happy, as was Jordan. And then she dropped a bombshell: Jordan's third name was... NORMAN. Jordan Terrance Norman. The synchronicity of all this astounds me to this day, and as I write this, I am overcome with emotion...

On March 6, 2006, Jordan had surgery to relieve the fluid around his brain. His eyesight had continued to deteriorate, and the doctors needed to place a permanent shunt in his brain. When Jordan woke up from his shunt surgery, he was laughing and giggling. As he recovered, all the students at our school continued to pray, make cards, write stories, and compose letters. Jordan amazed the doctors and nurses at Sick Kids, and the media personalities who visited the hospital.

Everyone was ecstatic when Jordan returned to our school in January 2007. He had finished his intensive treatment in September and would be able to continue oral chemotherapy treatments at home, with regular check-ups in Toronto and the help of a special educator for the partially sighted.

In June 2015, I bumped into Jordan's mom after taking my mother to an appointment. Jordan had graduated from Grade 8 and had received an award. She proudly showed me some photos and later emailed them to me.

Occasionally, I think about Jordan and NORMAN the GOOD NEWS BEAR™, and the little prayer that came with him: "The Lord is my strength and my shield; My heart trusts in Him, and I am helped." (Psalm 28:7, NAS)

Jordan and NORMAN helped *me* to believe in miracles!

Nutella—Worth Its Weight In Gold

I admire mother and daughter teams who go shopping together, or out to the occasional movie and restaurant... They are comfortable in their respective roles, yet there exists another dimension to their relationship. They can play together and have fun while they spend an afternoon engrossed in heavy-duty retail therapy.

Shopping with my mother, I recall, chuckling, was not always what I would call therapeutic. If anything, I felt I would greatly benefit from therapy *after* a few hours of shopping with her.

Don't get me wrong—I loved Ma—but sometimes she could be a bit much. Despite being small in stature, she took up a big part of my life, and even more so after Dad passed. Not that I minded, most of the time. Case in point, we often cooked together: first, because I knew she was lonely, and second, I was determined that she pass on to me every Calabrian dish she had learned from *her* mother. If we were not cooking together, we'd often watch cooking shows, sitting side by side in matching armchairs.

I blame Ma for getting me hooked on *Iron Chef America*. There was one episode where eels were the featured item, and Ma's eyes lit up. She recounted how they used to enjoy them back in the old country, and she laughed when I cringed and declared that I could never eat such a snake-like creature.

And then there were the comedy shows. *The Golden Girls*, *Everybody Loves Raymond*, and even the older ones, like *Bewitched*. They brought laughter into her life—and mine—and our grief over the loss of Dad was assuaged for a while.

But I digress. It's shopping with Ma that tested my patience.

One Sunday, the grocery store was packed with the after-Mass shoppers navigating their carts with post-eucharistic vigour. Holy Rollers, I thought, chuckling inwardly. Having done their spiritual duty, they could now proceed with grocery duty. My mother, oblivious to one and all, took her time. I expended a considerable amount of energy helping her guide her cart around to avoid collisions as she fished out the biggest watermelon from the bin, chose the best bunches of rapini, loaded up with olive oil and tomato *passata* on sale, and added anything she felt needed replenishing in her cupboards, basement kitchen, and in her *cantina*. I knew that if a world crisis occurred, I could flee to Ma's place; we'd have everything we needed for months.

Afterwards, Ma and I went shopping for gifts for some relatives in Italy. First, we went to a department store where she occasionally bought gold when it was *haffa*-price. There were no specials on, but she looked through the glass displays of bracelets, chains, earrings, and pendants anyway. "How much *is*?" she asked over and over in her faltering English, which came out more like "How much *eez*?" Ma then pointed to the crucifixes. One had a tiny body of Jesus on a simple cross, and two were so thin that they looked like crisscrossed nails. "I take that one for my nephew," my mother said, choosing the former for my cousin Franco, and then decided on a thicker one for his wife. "Now, something for the children..." Ma's eyes lit up when she spotted another crucifix. Again, a satisfied nod.

Three down, one more to go, I thought, checking the time. With any luck, I'd be home in time for a late lunch.

The delay came when she tried to decide on earrings for her sixteen-year-old great-niece. "I no like," she declared when I made several suggestions. Exasperated, I said, "Ma, you're seventy-eight years old and you're trying to buy earrings for a sixteen-year-old. Trust me, she's going to like these." I pointed to a pair made up of various sized intertwining loops.

"I dunno," she murmured. "They no shine like 14 carat gold... Okay, I take," she said finally.

When I returned home, my head was pulsating with the beginning of a migraine. I trudged into the kitchen and wearily opened the fridge, hoping to find something to give me a miraculous boost of energy. Salad? No, it looked as wilted as I felt. Organic carrots? No, it would take too much energy to munch them. I sighed, closed the door and shuffled to the pantry. My eyes scanned the shelves desperately; I needed *something* that would restore me.

Ahh, of course! My eyes rested on an extra-large, 750 ml jar of pure restorative... Nutella! Chocolate *and* hazelnuts? I was too weak to resist. In a sudden jolt of energy, I grabbed the jar, reached for a spoon, and then plopped myself into a chair. Normally I would have spread some on a toasted slice of bread—it made the Nutella melt into gooey heaven—but I had already decided to forego this step and instead enjoy an instant boost.

As the velvety mixture embraced my taste buds, I shut my eyes in satisfaction. I deserved this reward, I reasoned, for surviving the morning. Exactly the therapy I needed.

ꝺ

Later that evening, Ma called to tell me that the chain for her nephew's wife was not long enough.

"Ma, it fit me okay," I sighed.

"But it was hard to open and close."

I *had* struggled with the clasp. "I have fat fingers, Ma. And she's smaller than I am. It'll fit her perfectly."

"There's a sale on gold tomorrow. I want you to bring me downtown. I want to get a new chain."

"Ma, there's nothing wrong with the one you have, for God's sake."

"Ah, *Madonna*, don't get me upset," she warned.

My mouth snapped shut. Her underlying message hit me like a *caciocavallo*: Don't argue with me, because I'll end up getting heartburn and maybe another heart attack...

I moaned inwardly. Italian mothers *always* know how and when to push that guilt button. "Fine," I heard myself muttering.

The next morning it was cloudy and humid. "These knees," she complained in our dialect, as she stepped down awkwardly from her doorstep to the ramp. As her ice-tipped fingers closed around my arm, I began my usual silent incantation to God to help me deal with Ma's excruciatingly slow pace, the result of two debilitating heart attacks and advanced osteoarthritis. Her cardiologist had warned her that she could no longer manipulate any stairs. This had just about killed my mother; she, like many Italians, depended on her basement kitchen for frying veal cutlets, and making sausages, lasagna, and tomato preserves.

I stopped suddenly. "Ma, did you remember your spray?"

She nodded, and I uttered yet another prayer that she wouldn't get heartburn, for which she would have to follow a protocol: *Spray once. Wait five minutes. If the heartburn persists, spray again. Wait another five minutes. If it still hasn't gone away, spray again and call 911.* This whole business scared the red blood cells right out of me, especially whenever I took Ma to see the doctor or to get blood work done. Or go shopping. I imagined scenes of congested traffic while she was spraying her third shot of nitro.

At the mall, Ma spotted the gold vendor. "He always make me good deal," she declared.

The vendor smiled, recognizing my mother, who made a point of telling him that she hadn't come by for a few years because of her two heart attacks. "My heart no good," she shrugged, and after his concerned reply, she began her exploration of his wares. "How much? Is 14 carat? You give-a-me *good price*? I buy *lotsa* gold here, remember?"

Finally, *finally*, she found a tri-colour gold chain she liked. She hesitated when he revealed the price. "I pay cash," Ma lowered her voice. "How much?"

The vendor sighed and dropped the price. Ma gave a triumphant smile and pulled out a wad of bills. I exchanged a grin with the vendor.

The next day, I went over to help Ma pack up the gift boxes. When I opened the box with the chain for her nephew's wife, I was surprised to see that the tri-colour gold chain had been replaced by the original chain, the one that she thought was too short and too hard to open and close.

"The *tri-colore* one is better for a *young-a* person," she said casually. "I give it to one of the granddaughters for Christmas. Come on, after we finish, we watch *Everybody Love Raymon'*, okay?"

I opened my mouth and then closed it. If Ma was happy, that was all that mattered. I smiled and nodded. As I cut a length of white ribbon, I asked, "Hey, Ma, do you have any Nutella?"

Our Canada: Tomatoes, Red Peppers, And Maple Leaves

Of course, we all eventually learned to speak English after immigrating, some more than others. At home, our parents spoke to us in our Calabrese dialect, and eventually we learned a new language, "Italiese"—a mix of Italian and Canadian English. Usually this consisted of adding a vowel like O, A, or U to the end of an English word. So the word cake, which is *torta* in Italian, became *cake*-a; truck, which is *camion* in Italian, became *trocc*-u. Ginger ale became *ginger-*ella. You get the idea.

Now, spelling food items was a different matter. When Ma couldn't go grocery shopping for some reason, reading her grocery list always took some time. She spelled the words phonetically, so I eventually figured out that the word that she had written *musci rum*—that I first read as mushy rum—was mushy room, which translated to mushroom. At first, I couldn't understand why she'd ask for something mushy from the store. Then there was *siroline.* I'd pronounce it to myself in the way she would say it, *seero*-line, *seero*-line... then the lightbulb went on: sirloin!

Our mother could multitask before the word became commonplace. She cooked, sewed, knit, and crocheted while the televised drama unfolded in Santa Barbara or Genoa City. Our mother learned these fine arts back in the old country. She could replicate a complicated sweater or dress pattern by looking at any picture. She never needed written instructions. With perfect stitching, she made dresses, pants, coats, and hats with pompoms the size of meatballs. *Big* meatballs. While she watched Nikki and Victor get married for the seventh time, she managed to make stuffed peppers, or *bistecca alla pizzaiola*, or a pot of tomato sauce and meatballs. Most of the time, the aromas in the house when we got home from school made our mouths water and we'd run to the kitchen. On occasion, when she decided to make *trippa* or *baccalà*, we wanted to run away. No tripe or codfish for us!

Ma had this thing about salt. In 2007, after having two heart attacks, her cardiologist warned her to stay away from it. He didn't understand that telling that to an Italian was like saying: Never eat salami or pasta or tomato sauce. *Ever!*

Did Ma salt her food? Of course she did. She always claimed that she used hardly enough to taste. But I guess the amount she put into her cooking made her what she was—salt of the earth.

Ma wanted the best for her family in Canada. And although it sometimes saddened her that she and Dad didn't have the means in those early years to provide us with what she would have liked, she always provided. And she was happy to give her grandchildren what she couldn't give us at the time.

But Ma, you've given us more than enough. You taught us how to provide for our children, how to celebrate our Italian heritage, how to make a great tomato sauce.

You occasionally cursed Christopher Columbus for having discovered America—the 40-below winters might have been the cause—but yours and Dad's sacrifice to leave Italy and immigrate to Canada was a gift to us. A gift of two cultures and two languages. We are all proud of our Italian heritage and we are certainly very proud of being Canadian. And for years, we noticed that you always placed the Canadian flag insert from the newspaper in your front window on Canada Day. We're all proud of you, Ma.

Life was not easy for you at times. Life was tough, but you were tough, too. Tough enough to keep on going eight years after two major heart attacks.

And so, when I was deciding what to wear for your funeral service, Ma, I chose a black dress and a red shawl. Black to respect our Italian tradition and red to symbolize love. Your love for your family and our love for you. Red to represent our Canadian flag and the beautiful maple leaves in the fall. Red to represent the glorious tomato and the hundreds, maybe thousands of pots of tomato sauce you made over your lifetime. And red for the red peppers you fried and left on the counter for us a few hours before you joined Pina and Dad in heaven.

Thank you, Ma. They were delicious.

The Sense Of It All...

She stares at me sometimes from behind her front window. I see the slight ripple of the silk curtain. I wait for her hands to appear and nudge it aside, but she doesn't always want to be seen.

I slowly drive by her house today and decide to stop. She's tending the patch of poppies in her side yard. I roll down my window, but she doesn't notice me.

She gives an irritated groan as she slowly unbends, rubbing her arthritic knees. She looks up into the cherry tree that's ripe with berries before shifting her gaze to the ground, the red-tinged pits studding the grass and concrete walkway. She mumbles, "Those damn birds, making such a mess, because I don't have enough work to do around here!" And then she gives a dismissive wave. "I suppose they have to eat, too..."

She shuffles to the back, where her bean and basil plants await their daily watering. Then she sets down her watering can, plods up the ramp to the side door, and enters. Moments later, I see her behind the curtain. This time her hands appear, and my hands tremble slightly at the wheel. I feel a sting behind my eyelids as my gaze shifts to the SOLD sign in the front yard, and I wonder who will be keeping a garden now. Next to the sign, the peonies are just about to bloom. I can almost smell their candy-sweet fragrance. My gaze shifts back to the window.

My mother's hands are gone.

Soon, the curtains will probably be gone, too.

I stare at the silk flowers on the passenger seat. My throat constricts as I head to the cemetery, leaving the chirping birds to their cherry feast.

It All Started With My Mother Tongue

The Impact Of Language On My Career As A Teacher And Writer

Doesn't everything start with your mother tongue? Does your mother tongue not forge the first relationships in your life? Does it not act as a metaphorical umbilical cord between you and your parents?

My mother tongue is the southern Italian dialect known as *Caminotu,* spoken in the mountainside village of Camini, in the region of Reggio Calabria. Camini was and remains a small community only seven kilometres from the Ionian Sea, with a thousand-plus-year history that includes Greek colonization—a significant influence that marked the land and its inhabitants to such an extent that the area became known as *Magna Grecia,* "Greater Greece." In fact, the name Camini derives from the Greek for "hearth" or "fireplace."

My mother's maiden name was Adavastro, a name that was Italianized during the period of Greek colonization from the original name Adamaster. According to a story that has been passed on over the centuries, my mother's ancestors were Greek warriors, *Guerrieri della tempesta*, "Warriors of the Storm."

Three years after I was born, my parents joined the thousands of other southern Italians who made the difficult decision to leave their beloved but impoverished homeland and seek a better life for their family overseas. We landed in Halifax in April 1963 and arrived by train in Sudbury on the first of May. Our family consisted of my parents, my older sister, my younger brother, and me. My mother was expecting her fourth child.

We settled in Gatchell, a neighbourhood with clusters of Italian immigrants. My father found employment with Inco, the International Nickel Company. When I was five, I started kindergarten at St. Anthony's School, situated steps away from where we lived. I didn't know a word of English. I don't think my parents prepared me for the fact that the teacher would be speaking another language.

The language issue in my life marked me on that first day of school. What an impact! The moment is etched in my mind and is one of my clearest early childhood memories.

I remember being in a classroom and the teacher was smiling. What remains foremost in my memory is the fact that the teacher spoke words to me that were strange. I didn't understand those words that sounded nothing like the *Caminotu* dialect I had been using in the first five years of my life.

Did I respond? I can't remember. But I do know that my blonde-haired teacher, Mrs. Piquette, had me sit apart from the others for a short time. She was kind to me. But with my five-year-old mentality and sensitivity, the moments I spent separated from the others had an indelible effect on me and made me feel *different.* Perhaps some of the other children of immigrants had minimal knowledge or comprehension of English. I don't know. But something stuck in my childhood psyche during that brief separation period. I felt confused, alone in a world that separated me because of my language, my mother tongue. I could no longer communicate in the way I had been raised. At least not at school.

Perhaps my desire to join the group, to understand and be understood, was my impetus to learn English quickly. I recall speaking to the teacher in English in Grade 1, telling her about the boy at the desk behind me who was tugging my hair. In Grade 2, I loved reading simple books and looked forward to our visits to the school library. On one occasion that year, I wanted to borrow *The Yearling,* a novel by Marjorie Kinnan Rawlings. I was captivated by the cover: a child embracing a fawn. It was somewhat advanced, at four hundred pages, for a seven-year-old. I discovered years later that it was a Pulitzer Prize winner, and in my early twenties, I actually found a pristine copy with the same cover at the World's Biggest Bookstore in Toronto.

My fascination with Rawlings and her books stayed with me, and after retiring from teaching in 2015, I visited her home in Cross

Creek, Florida. I was delighted to walk through the rooms where she had written her masterpiece—the novel that had captivated me at seven years of age—and other works.

By Grade 2, I felt much more comfortable with the English language and decided I wanted to become a teacher like my lovely and cheerful Mrs. Petrilli at St. Anthony's School (and later, like my other wonderful and dedicated elementary teachers Mrs. Degan, Mrs. Minniti, and Mrs. Bartolucci, with whom I am friends and still in touch). I was also inspired by my English teacher Mrs. Lalonde in Grade 8 at St. Francis School, where I was entranced by her lesson of "The Highwayman" by Alfred Noyes. Reading the ballad still gives me goosebumps. (I have thought about adapting it as a historical novel.)

As time passed, I became more serious about becoming a teacher, and my parents happily supported me in my aspirations. By the end of Grade 5, I determined that my younger brothers, Cosimo and Pasquale—six and eight, respectively, then—would make perfect practice students. So my father would call them in from their road hockey game and I proceeded to teach them religion or some other subject in our basement. I'm sure they were far from thrilled. I had them draw pictures, which I would subsequently mark, reward with a star, and then display on the basement walls.

At age eleven, I received what I thought was the best birthday present a girl could ever hope for—a big blackboard with a box of chalk! I had the tools I needed for my chosen profession. Now I could *really* practise with my brothers. I remember using that blackboard even in my last years of high school while studying for exams. Whether I was reviewing the biological life cycle of some species or outlining the position of various European countries during World War II, my trusty blackboard was always there.

Grade 5 was a pivotal year for me when it came to language. In September 1969, my mother took us back to Italy. We stayed until March 1970, and I found out only many years later that my mother was considering having us move back to Camini permanently. During that time, we went to school in Camini. My sister and I were initially placed in Grade 1 to become familiar with the standard Italian language. How awkward it was to be in a class with children four years younger than me. All the students spoke dialect at home, but formal schooling was conducted in standard Italian. I found myself in a kind of spotlight once again, with language being the major issue. There were many words that were close enough to my dialect to understand, but I didn't have the ability to speak standard Italian easily or to make myself understood. It felt like I was learning a new language again. Like my experience in kindergarten, I felt different and separated from the main group.

As the months progressed, we were fast-tracked to Grade 5, but I still recall feeling self-conscious when asked to reply or read a poem aloud in class, always wondering if my pronunciation was correct.

We returned to Sudbury at the end of March 1970. After a seven-month absence, I managed to surprise Mrs. Eaton with my ability to catch up. However, that year, a new program was introduced in the schools: Core French. I had missed seven months of daily French instruction. So I began learning yet another language, and since my classmates were ahead, I initially felt somewhat disadvantaged.

But I caught up with French, too. And as I was learning French, my English continued to strengthen. I read voraciously. I fondly recall the Bookmobile, a huge transport truck that rolled into our neighbourhood every Wednesday afternoon. The driver would park across from Albert's Grocery Store and set up the steps to this mobile public library. I was often the first one there after school. Watching this process was as exciting as entering and seeing all the book-lined shelves.

What a delight to have the chance to borrow books on a weekly basis. I brought home a dozen books and read them all. My mother despaired for my eyesight. "You'll need glasses if you keep reading that much," she warned. How sad for me and many others when the Bookmobile service was reduced to every second week before finally being terminated while I was in high school.

At Marymount High School, I excelled in my Italian, Latin, and French courses. I decided to major in Italian and French in my post-secondary Arts education at Laurentian University in Sudbury. I also studied Spanish and German, then graduated in 1980. I obtained my Bachelor of Education degree at Nipissing University in North Bay in 1981. While enrolled in additional university courses at Laurentian, I met up again with Mrs. Eaton, my

Grade 5 teacher, who was taking "The Development of Western Morality" along with me. We ended up collaborating on a project, and it was a most enjoyable endeavour. It was wonderful getting to know her as an adult, as I had only been in her class for a little over three months when I was ten.

During my elementary teaching career, I taught every grade, with most of my years focused on teaching junior and senior kindergarten, in both the English and French Immersion programs. I developed many successful strategies for a strong foundation in literacy and have shared my ideas and program by giving workshops to teachers in Sudbury and across Ontario. I received four Best Practice Awards from OECTA, the Ontario Elementary Catholic Teachers Association, for my literacy and other initiatives. I truly believe that my experiences with language and my culture were instrumental in my formation and success as a teacher.

Early in life, I decided I wanted to help others learn, perhaps because *I* needed help to learn. Most of my career was dedicated to helping children learn a second language. Teaching language involves a sensitivity that I felt I had because of my heritage and my personal experiences with language learning. When I introduced these children to the new language, I recalled the day I was separated and didn't understand a word of English. I didn't want any of my students to feel isolated, confused, different, or uncomfortable, as I initially did.

My experiences with my language and cultural heritage have influenced me not only as an educator, but as a writer. Many of the short stories I've written explore the themes of my heritage. Fascinated with the history of my homeland, I had purchased a suitcase full of books during a trip to Calabria, and as I read, I was inspired to bring the turbulent period of post-Unification history to life, because it was—and is—a part of my family history. After many years of research and writing, my historical novel *La Brigantessa* was published.

In a sense, I have come full circle, studying the culture and language I was born into, and exploring the Greek origins of my dialect, a valid language in its own right.

Language must be uttered to live. I am proud to add my *Caminotu* dialect to the list of languages I have learned over the years and continue to study. It's an inextricable part of my identity. In my vocation as a teacher, I loved to play with language, and in my other passion as a writer, I derive much pleasure from playing with words. I may have been silent for a while in kindergarten, but eventually learned how to loosen my tongue, as my mother jokingly remarked.

What can I say? It all started with my mother tongue.

Exploring My Italian Heritage Through Writing

Writing is not something I undertook as someone might a new hobby or sport. For me, writing became an exercise in self-expression and self-discovery, to lift the fog from my perception of my identity. Why did I need to discover myself, why did I feel the need to explore my feelings about my identity? What *was* my identity? At thirty-five years of age, I asked myself, *am I experiencing a so-called identity crisis?*

I came to realize, through much introspection, that my past was catching up to me, that my "Italian heritage" was seeking re-birth, so to speak, in my consciousness—a consciousness that had, since my immigration to Canada at three years of age, gone through subtle and perhaps not so subtle mutations in the process of becoming "Canadian."

As an immigrant, I had experienced displacement and had spent many years living in a culture within another culture. Only an immigrant can truly understand this duality and the specific feelings that are engendered because of it: the feeling of being different, of not being understood, of being inferior, of growing up trying to *integrate,* and perhaps sometimes attempting to *assimilate* into the Canadian tapestry.

Joseph Pivato states that "our immigrant experience is our first major confrontation with the contradictions of life, with different realities. We are forced to live and work in two worlds."* Like many immigrants I had to ask myself, *am I Italian? Am I Canadian? Could I quantify which percentage of my being was Italian, which percentage was Canadian?*

I concluded that some of the answers that I was seeking would come to me through research. I needed to understand where I came from. I needed to rediscover my roots and explore my heritage, and through that figure out their importance in forming my identity and my spirit.

I began my homework. One of the first books that enlightened me was called *Such Hardworking People* by Franca Iacovetta. It was the study of the diaspora of Italians in Toronto. I was enraptured. Reading this book was like receiving a gift; the author's intensive research solidified and validated my history, my status as an immigrant, my identity. It fueled the spark already present within me and set it aflame.

---

* Joseph Pivato, "Nothing Left to Say: Italian-Canadian Writers," *Writers in Transition* (Montreal: Guernica Editions, 1990), p. 36

Along with reading, I began questioning. The questions were initially directed primarily to my parents, my closest link to my heritage. They readily provided me with answers, happy to embark on a reverse metaphorical journey to their homeland. I picked at their memories like an archeologist using her delicate tools to brush the dust and sand from a targeted site, growing in excitement as layers of time were swept away, ultimately revealing a concrete link to the past.

My heritage continued to beckon. Overwhelmed by nostalgia for my country of birth, I flew into her arms, figuratively and literally. I flew to Italy in the summer of 1998. My last visit to my native Calabria had been in the summer of 1974, and now I was returning after twenty-four years without my parents. I reunited with my relatives, re-establishing the ties that I had come to realize were still connected to me, having stretched beyond the Calabrian mountain ranges and Ionian Sea in an invisible yet tangible grip.

In Calabria, those ties strengthened, and I felt myself coming full circle. The Italian heritage which I had embraced tentatively growing up, and sometimes denied, as I attempted to become more "Canadian," I now accepted as an integral, inextricable part of me, not in any definable percentage, but fully absorbed in my being. And during this most revelatory trip, I discovered something surprising—I realized how very Canadian I was, a question I had grappled with as much as the question of my Italian identity. Yes, my heritage was proudly Italian, but at the same time, I was undeniably, and proudly Canadian.

I am Italian-Canadian. The knowledge that I could truly embrace both cultures and hold dual identities has brought me peace. I didn't have to pledge allegiance to just one at the expense of diminishing the other's importance—or even losing the other.

Joseph Pivato affirms that "immigration is the starting point for all our art. Our translocation is the beginning of our consciousness of the larger world outside our Italian villages, and the catalyst for our writing."*

My writing is an expression of my being, of my discoveries. In both fiction and non-fiction, I explore the themes inherent in heritage: family, history, beliefs and traditions, the immigrant experience, food, and landscape.

The ongoing process of examining my Italian and Canadian culture through research and writing has reinforced my understanding about myself as a woman, a mother, a sister, a wife... that is, my identity.

---

* Ibid, pp. 35-36

Writing Through Grief

Everyone processes grief in their own way. Over the years, while processing the losses in my life, I have inevitably put my thoughts, reflections, and emotions on paper, and have found that the mystical process of either writing longhand, or typing my sentiments on my computer, have produced a healing alchemy, a release, a necessary outlet for me to deal with emotions that have been too painful to share with even relatives or close friends.

The first time I wrote about a significant loss was in the early 1990s, in a story entitled "Angel of God," but the loss itself occurred in the mid-1970s. At seventeen years of age, my sister Giuseppina ("Pina") was diagnosed with stomach flu. My sister's abdominal pains continued and my parents brought her to hospital, where she was operated on immediately. We thought that she was recovering, but her fragile body had not been able to overcome the peritonitis from her ruptured appendix.

I had always been a highly sensitive child, and at fifteen years old my body and brain became numb from the news and at the scenes that were unfolding before me. I witnessed my parents' despair, the line of family friends at the funeral home, and the aftermath of this family tragedy which happened twelve years after we had immigrated from Italy. There was no one to talk to about our loss. No counselling. It was the mid-1970s, after all, and seeking an outside source other than a priest, perhaps, wouldn't have even been considered by my immigrant parents.

Years later, as I was processing another loss, the end of my first marriage, I often wished I had my sister in my life to share my feelings with, to cry on her shoulder, to express my sadness on being a single parent of two young children. I felt so alone.

I went on a weekend trip to a scenic island in northern Ontario with some girlfriends, and while the others were already in the main cabin for breakfast, I strangely felt my sister's presence while walking along the path to the cabin, the summer breeze carrying the scent of the pines and cedars around me.

We returned home the following day, and I couldn't get my sister out of my mind. I couldn't sleep that night. After midnight, I found myself heading to the computer, and the memories of that April afternoon came rushing back to me. As I typed, the tears started to flow as I recalled faces, voices, and emotions. Random memories I had buried, like the question one well-meaning relative had asked me, "Are you afraid to sleep in your bedroom tonight?" I'd shared the room with Pina. I'd said no. I recalled looking over at her bed, her clothes, at the tube of lip gloss she had left on the dresser.

I know I typed blind for a stretch—I didn't need to look at the keyboard—the tears flowing with every detail that sprang to my consciousness, every detail that my fifteen-year-old brain had safely stored away, unable to process it during the actual time of the event. As the words appeared on the page, the dam of emotions that had held together for years finally broke. The emotions were raw, the memories painful, the grief overwhelming, but when the story was done, the words out, the tears subsiding, I felt a burgeoning awareness: I had, after over fifteen years, finally mourned the loss of my sister. A few years later, in a moment of courage, I submitted my story to a journal—and it was published.

Three years later our family was dealing with the declining health of my father due to Parkinson's disease. He had been diagnosed in 1988, and by the mid-1990s his condition was worsening. Although he never exhibited the telltale shaking symptoms, his walking became stiff, his vision deteriorated, an eventual stroke left him speechless, and he lost his ability to remember, to walk, to feed himself. We lost him a little at a time.

I remember sitting at the kitchen table one day, when he was still able to play cards—he liked to play *briscola*—and he made a move that was puzzling. He was puzzled too, and I recall his own embarrassed laugh, and the card game ended early. I was initially shocked at this clear sign of what I learned was Parkinson's related dementia, but eventually it inspired me to write a story where the parent/child roles are reversed. When Dad had another episode that led to his hospitalization, I dealt with my inner grief and helplessness by writing about my visits to him. Later, after he suffered a stroke and was again in hospital, I wrote about the heart-wrenching experience of coming to terms with his compromised quality of life and his imminent death.

Again, as in the story about my sister, the words that were borne from these experiences were accompanied by tears, and in this case, anticipatory grief and deep sorrow. But in writing them down, I was allowing my emotions to be vented, for grief to flow outward with my tears, instead of releasing their toxins inside me.

Writing down my thoughts, my observations, and my emotions about sitting at my father's bedside in hospital, spooning the puréed peas into his mouth, cringing at the eggplant splotches on his wrists and arms from the various injections, helplessly gazing at the restraints at his wrists preventing him from pulling out the IV tube he needed when he could no longer manage to swallow... Each of these moments sank painfully into my mind and heart, initial imprints that somehow eventually made their way from the blood red recesses of my heart to the stark white expanse of the page, each word a testament to my father's life, validating his earthly experience. Later, when my stories were published, several readers expressed their gratitude to me for sharing and validating moments that they, too, had experienced, and for helping them release pent-up emotions.

Perhaps that was one of the reasons I wrote it out—I wanted to help myself deal with the trials of life, instinctively knowing that perhaps, one day, a reader would find solace in knowing that someone else had had a similar experience.

A sorrow shared is a sorrow lessened.

❧

My writing expanded into the realm of adult and children's fiction. I finished the manuscript for my first novel and began the research for my second. For decades I had invested in my growth as a writer: joining writers' groups, attending conferences, doing mentorships and a correspondence course at the Humber School for Writers, reading countless books on the art and craft of writing, getting my creative non-fiction published in over a dozen anthologies, all while teaching, raising a family (now blended after my remarriage), and dealing with the declining health and eventual passing of my beloved father and dear mother-in-law after her eight-month cancer ordeal.

I retired from teaching, one of my life-long passions, in June of 2015, happy with what I had contributed to education, knowing I had made an impact. I had received several Best Practice teaching awards over the years, but the personal rewards that I received from children, whose eyes had lit up during my lessons, whose creativity had been sparked, whose love of stories, books, and learning had manifested in so many ways, were countless. Angelica, one of my students in both junior and senior kindergarten, sought me out at the end of high school, saying that my stories and writing had inspired her to write poetry. Two other students—Megan and Laryssa—attended the launch of my children's book in 2019 with their own infants, looking for a copy of the book from the teacher who had shared with them her love of books and reading in their early years.

Having come to the end of one fulfilling career, I was now ready to embark on a full-time writing career, my other passion. I had finished a historical novel in 2012, invested in a manuscript evaluation, and worked on a subsequent draft. After participating in a weekend workshop in 2014, I continued polishing and revising. I was excited about the journey ahead, and at this point, wanted to ensure that my manuscript was the best that it could be before submitting it to publishers.

After retirement, however, life soon revealed that the journey ahead was not going to be a smooth one. My mother passed away in early September 2015, a few years after a couple of serious heart attacks. Four months later, our thirteen-year-old dog died. Two hard-hitting events that left me feeling as if I were in a turbulent ocean in a small boat without oars. I was engulfed in waves of grief. Then a close friend and neighbour died.

Immersing myself in my writing over the years has provided me with an escape from reality. Or, when the spirit has moved me to write about the actual experiences of loss, penning my thoughts and feelings helped me deal with reality and come to terms with loss and grief, ultimately moving towards acceptance, hope, and peace.

Eventually, the historical novel that I wrote and researched over many years—*La Brigantessa*—was published by Inanna Publications of Toronto in 2018.

There have been other significant losses in recent years, the most heartbreaking being the loss of my beloved son-in-law, Alain, in 2018. As a respite from the constant grief and sleepless nights, I immersed myself in my writing...

In the span of five years, Harlequin UK published five of my romance novels, Pajama Press of Toronto published two of my children's books, and Inanna published a collection called *Pigeon Soup & Other Stories*. Since then, I have completed a sequel to *La Brigantessa,* penned another romance novel for Harlequin, and I've compiled several of my personal stories in this collection.

I continue to allow my writing to guide me through difficult and challenging times. Whether I'm inspired to write about meatballs, migration, or other memories, this is something that I must do...

Open my heart and tell my story.

Acknowledgements

Having written a story a few years ago called "Product of Italy/Made in Canada"—which is how I saw and still see myself—I felt it would make a perfect addition and title for this collection, where I share my pride in my Italian roots and in my adoptive country.

I would like to express my gratitude and appreciation to the following:

To my husband Nic and our family, immediate and extended, for their love and support. *La famiglia* is everything to me.

To my late parents, Carmela and Nicola Micelotta, who, in making the difficult decision to immigrate from Italy, ultimately raised me and my siblings with our valued Calabrese traditions while allowing us to become who we are as proud Canadians, celebrating our dual identities.

To Heather Campbell for publishing this book. Since 2015, when she founded Latitude 46 Publishing with Laura Gregorini, and after assuming full ownership in 2019, Heather has continued to elevate the literary arts in Northern Ontario, enhancing the public's awareness and appreciation of the works of regional writers. She has published close to 50 titles in ten years. I am honoured to have my book join these fine titles.

To Randall Perry, editor extraordinaire, whose keen eye and brilliant insights and suggestions truly elevated my work. It was a pleasure and a privilege to work with him.

To Sabrina Futia for her discerning copy-editing in the final preparation of the manuscript for publication.

To my friends and colleagues in my professional writer groups: the SWG (Sudbury Writers' Guild), the AICW (Association of Italian-Canadian Writers) and my weekly AICW "Write Time" group, the CAA (Canadian Authors Association and the CAA Toronto Branch), TWUC (The Writers' Union of Canada), and the IAWA (Italian American Writers Association) for supporting me and my work in various ways throughout the years.

To the Canada Council for the Arts, Ontario Arts Council, Access Copyright, and the Public Lending Right for championing the rights of writers and their works.

To Vicki Gilhula, who started the Sudbury Writers' Guild in 1992—which I immediately joined—and who, the year before, held a writing course where I received early encouragement, and where I wrote a version of my "Nonna" story.

To friend and author Maria Coletta McLean, who read my very first published story almost 30 years ago and reached out via email to tell me how much she enjoyed it, encouraging me to continue to write. And to all my friends, near and far, for their support over the years.

To Angie and Regan, for their longtime friendship and hospitality at their lovely camp on the French River, a place that always inspires me as a writer.

To Dr. Joseph Pivato, Professor Emeritus, Literary Studies at Athabasca University, who, as indicated in Wikipedia, "first established the critical recognition of Italian-Canadian literature and changed perceptions of Canadian writing." His publications are numerous and significant.

To the endorsers of this book:

Elio Iannacci, award-winning writer, poet, and long-time arts reporter for *The Globe and Mail*, with contributions to 80 publications worldwide, including *Vogue Italia*, *The Hollywood Reporter*, *The Toronto Review of Books*, and many major Canadian newspapers, for his perceptive and gracious endorsement.

Dr. Gabriel Niccoli, Professor Emeritus, University of Waterloo, editor of *Ricordi: Racconti di vite oltreoceano* and *Patterns of Nostos in Italian Canadian Narratives*, for his encouragement and validation of my stories of our shared Calabrian heritage and Italian-Canadian experience.

Sonia Saikaley, 2020 Gold IPPY Award winner of *The Allspice Bath,* for her sensitivity of cultural identity and immigrant spirit and themes, not only in my stories, but in her books *The Lebanese Dishwasher* and *The Allspice Bath,* and her children's book, *Samantha's Sandwich Stand.*

To the teachers who have inspired me over the years to choose teaching as a vocation. Teaching was always a passion for me, along with reading and writing.

To the students I specifically wrote about in this book: Jordan, Teshaylia, and "Robert," all of whom taught me invaluable lessons during my career, along with the other dear students I've mentioned, and all my students over the years. Each and every one of you was a gift to me.

To the Calabria Social Club and the *Società* Caruso Club of Sudbury (and its Culture & Education Committee with Director Diana Iuele-Colilli) for their long-time support.

To Cosimo Micelotta, General Manager of Journal Printing, Sudbury, for his support and generous sponsorship of publicity materials for this book.

And finally, to *you*, dear Reader. May these stories resonate with you, make you laugh, touch your heart, and perhaps inspire you to write your own stories.

Permissions

Time to Say Goodbye: Lyrics from the song "Time to Say Goodbye (Con te partirò)" (Sartori - Quarantotto – Peterson © Sugar s.r.l. – Double Marpot s.r.l. Used by permission.

Bears and Good News: The real names of the people in this story are used by permission. NORMAN and THE GOOD NEWS BEARS™ and all related product quotes © Amy Wulfing. Used by permission.

Nutella—Worth its Weight in Gold: NUTELLA® is a trademark of Ferrero S.p.A. Used by permission.

Previous Appearances

Many of the stories in this collection have appeared in earlier versions in the following publications:

"Illumination" was published in Vol. 32 (2018) *Italian Canadiana: Italians in Canada: 150+ Years*, edited by Diana Iuele-Colilli and Christine Sansalone.

"Product of Italy/Made in Canada" was published in the AICW (Association of Italian-Canadian Writers) Anniversary Anthology *People, Places, Passages: An Anthology of Canadian Writing*, published in 2018 by Longbridge Books, edited by Giulia De Gasperi, Delia De Santis, and Caroline Morgan Di Giovanni.

A version of "The Immigrants, 1963" appeared in 2018 as "The Newcomers," a short story in Latitude 46 Publishing's *150 Years Up North and More*, edited by Karen McCauley and Laura Stradiotto.

"Learning My Lesson" was published in 2017 in *Chicken Soup for the Soul: Inspiration for Teachers*, edited by Amy Newmark and Alex Kajitani.

"You Are What You... Wear" appeared in 2010 as a short story in *Gathered Streams, A Canadian Authors Association Toronto Branch Anthology*, published by Hidden Brook Press, edited by Sharon Crawford, Jake Hogeterp and Nathan Medcalf.

"Angel of God" appeared in 2007 as a short story in Canadian Woman Studies' special issue, *Women Writing 3: Journeys*, published by Inanna Publications and Education Inc., edited by Frances Beer, Brenda Cranney, Andrea Medovarski, and Luciana Ricciutelli.

"It All Started with my Mother Tongue: The Impact of Language on My Career as Teacher and Writer" appeared in 2007 as an essay in *After the Years of Immigration: The Lives of Italian-Canadians*, published by Editions Soleil Publishing Inc., edited by Diana Iuele-Colilli.

"Time to Say Goodbye..." was published in 2006 as a short story in *Stumbling Through Darkness*, published by Wingate Press, edited by Stacey Newman.

"Cycles" and "Daddy's Girl" appeared in 2003 as short stories in *WORDSCAPE 8*, published by the Canadian Authors Association (Toronto Branch), edited by Sharon Crawford and Maryan Gibson.

"Exploring My Italian Heritage Through Writing" was published in 2002 as an essay in *The Harvest of a New Life: Documenting, Thinking and Representing the Italian-Canadian Experience*, published by Editions Soleil Publishing Inc., edited by Diana Iuele-Colilli.

A multiple award-winning teacher and writer, Rosanna Micelotta Battigelli was born in Calabria, Italy, and immigrated to Sudbury, Ontario with her family at three years of age. During her teaching career, she received four OECTA (Ontario English Catholic Teachers' Association) Best Practice Awards for her unique strategies in early literacy and other initiatives, including "Helping Pupils Who Grieve." Rosanna is a professional member of The Writers' Union of Canada (TWUC), the Canadian Authors Association (CAA), the Association of Italian-Canadian Writers (AICW), the Italian American Writers Association (IAWA New York/ Boston), the Canadian Society of Children's Authors, Illustrators, & Performers (CANSCAIP), the Toronto Romance Writers (TRW), and the Sudbury Writers' Guild, her first group, of which she has been Past President for two years and a member since 1992. Rosanna has also held a position on the Wordstock Sudbury Literary Festival Board, the AICW Executive Committee, the Calabria Social Club Board of Directors, and the Culture & Education Committee of the Società Caruso Club. Over the years, she has mentored both teachers and emerging writers.

An alumna of the Humber School for Writers, Rosanna has been published in twenty anthologies and journals and has read at many conferences and literary events in Canada, New York, and Italy. Her novel, *La Brigantessa* (Inanna Publications, 2018), was awarded a 2019 Gold IPPY Award for Historical Fiction, and was a finalist for both the CAA Fred Kerner Book Award and the Northern Lit Award in 2019. It also received an Honourable Mention at the 2024 Hollywood Book Festival, "celebrating books that deserve greater recognition from the film, television, and gaming industries" (Hollywood Book Festival website). Rosanna has since written the sequel to *La Brigantessa*, as yet unpublished. *Pigeon Soup & Other Stories* (Inanna, 2021) was honoured as a finalist in the Fiction: Short Story category of the 2021 American BookFest Best Book Awards and the 2022 International Book Awards.

Along with writing historical fiction, short fiction, and creative non-fiction, Rosanna has had six romance novels published with Harlequin/Mills & Boon (HarperCollins) and two children's books published with Pajama Press. Rosanna lives in Sudbury with her husband in a house full of books. When she is not reading, researching, or writing, she is making her family's favourite Calabrese dishes, and reading or cooking with her eight-year-old granddaughter Rosalie, who has already garnered numerous certificates for the *frittata* and other dishes she made at "The Battigelli Culinary Institute." (A cookbook may be one of Rosanna's future projects!)

More about Rosanna's publications can be found at www.rosannabattigelli.com.